Good or Bad Design?

Scandinavia has produced more good design in the last
forty years than the rest of Europe and America put
together. In this book Odd Brochmann, a distinguished
Norwegian architect, supplies a guide to just what good
(and bad) design is all about. He discusses the concepts of
the ugly and the good-looking, what makes some things
attractive and others repulsive, and to what extent our
reactions are linked with, and so limited by, period and
circumstances, or are of more enduring validity.
Understanding these things enables the architect or
designer to work with increased awareness towards
creating a stimulating environment; it endows the layman
with a capacity for genuine choice in shaping his
immediate private environment.

   Good or Bad Design? is a basic text intended
principally for secondary school students. It is also for
everyone interested in his surroundings. This refreshing
book will provide many pointers to what is or is not
good design.

Good or Bad Design?

by Odd Brochmann

translated by Maurice Michael

Studio Vista: London
Van Nostrand Reinhold Company: New York

A Studio Vista/Van Nostrand Reinhold Art Paperback
Edited by John Lewis
© this English translation Maurice Michael 1970
Published in London by Studio Vista Limited
Blue Star House, Highgate Hill, London N19
and in New York by Van Nostrand Reinhold Company
450 West 33 Street, New York, NY 10001
Library of Congress Catalog Card Number: 79–126306
Set in 11 pt Baskerville 1 pt leaded
Printed and bound in the Netherlands
by Drukkerij Reclame N.V., Gouda
British SBN paperback 289 70042 6
              hardback 289 70043 4

Contents

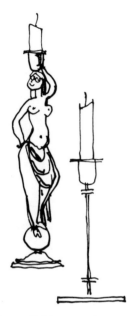

The shape of objects can be
conceived in a variety of ways

What is ugly and what is good-looking?

Imagine a design student, a girl let us say, searching for
a subject for her diploma thesis. She is sitting in a bus one
morning, about the time when housewives are setting out
to do their shopping. She starts looking at the hats the
other women are wearing and gets a surprise. She is surprised first of all that there should be so many different
and even strange forms of headgear, and that these must
all have been made by people and that these people must
be assumed to have *meant* something by making them in
that way.

Stranger still is the thought that these hats can scarcely
have been distributed haphazard to their wearers, but
presumably were chosen freely and even wanted. What
our student finds more difficult to understand is what
decided these choices, because most of them are anything
but convincing.

Now, women's hats are among the things that are
meant to satisfy certain practical needs along with certain
spiritual ones. At all events, the original idea was that a
hat should shelter the crown of the head and protect it
from sun and rain. It is also accepted as a general requirement that a hat should look well both in itself and in
conjunction with its wearer. In other words it comes
within the province of the designer. And so our student
continued to ponder this question of hats and eventually
arrived at the following analysis of the women's choices:

1. Some, or rather one, had obviously made her choice
with the hat's utilitarian qualities in mind.
2. Some, two in fact, had shown a well-developed sense
for what was pretty and becoming. But the fact that the
two hats in question were essentially different while the
wearers were relatively similar in appearance, provided
material for further thought.

3. Some had chosen their hats because they (rightly) were expensive – without this necessarily meaning that they wanted to make a display of their wealth.

4. Some had done the opposite and chosen their hat because it was cheap – without this necessarily meaning that they were hard up.

5. Some had made their choice without actually deciding whether the hat was pretty or not, they chose it because they thought it corresponded to the fashion or their women friends' interpretation of it, or, not feeling sure of themselves, they had let themselves be guided by the saleswoman's judgment and advice.

6. Very few can have been guided solely by one of the considerations mentioned. To some extent they will all have been complementary.

Having reached this stage, one can imagine the student stopping to examine her own reactions to the hats and reaching these two conclusions:

7. The two hats that I thought pretty were obviously worn by people from my own milieu; and although I think that I understand these matters it may well be that my judgment of them was affected by this fact. So, if the other women are satisfied with their hats and their friends also approve of them, what right have *I* to set myself up in judgment?

8. The hats in paintings from former times never seem ugly or funny to me, yet many modern ones do. Is that because people's sense of the beautiful has regrettably deteriorated for one reason or another, or is my attitude here determined by other factors?

This book will attempt to deal with these phenomena and the questions raised in these eight points; that is to say: why we shape things and react to their appearance and character as we do.

Strangely enough, where there is a question of what is called taste, many people regard it as admirable to have a narrow, uncompromising attitude, as if that were evidence of a well thought out personal view; whereas in reality such an attitude is mostly based on purely fortuitous circumstances and as a result, makes for more

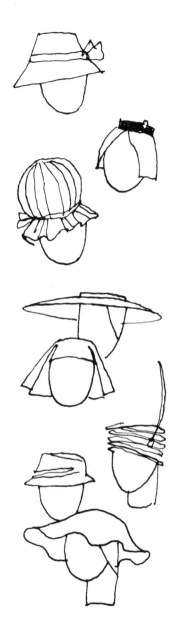

What is going on in her head?

Were hats prettier in 1530?

unpleasantness and less pleasure. A person who only likes fish and chips is perhaps less fortunate than someone who can take pleasure in fine cooking and who has also developed a sense of how the various raw materials can be prepared to bring out the best in them. Without that knowledge he will never be able to know which are the foodstuffs that give him the greatest sense of well being.

Whatever you are concerned with, thought and an open eye for all the possibilities can only be enriching. The wider the perspective, the stronger our *experience,* and it is really experience that we are after. Preferably in everyday things.

Our strongest experiences in relation to things made by other people occur with art, but to explain why and how lies outside the scope of this book. Here we are only concerned with the ugly and the good-looking, with what makes some things repulsive and others attractive, to what extent our reactions are linked with period and circumstances or are of more enduring validity. Understanding these things enables the architect or designer to work with increased awareness towards creating a stimulating environment; while for the layman, that is for everyone else, it is essential for him to be able to *choose* systematically when shaping his more immediate private surroundings. Systematically in this context means in accordance with one's circumstances, one's views and one's attitude to life generally.

Le Corbusier: a pioneer in the use of space.

The sensible hat

It might be said that the woman who chose her hat because of its serviceability and did not allow her emotions or circumstances to dictate to her was ruled by common sense. Let us for the time being by-pass questions as to whether the hat she chose was the most sensible one to choose and to what extent it could on this basis be called good-looking.

The primary function of the hat is the most obvious here – it is a *tool*. Ordinarily we regard as tools only those things that are used in connection with some kind of work, but most of the things with which we surround ourselves really belong to the same category. Apart from decorations and pure *objets d'art* the rest of our belongings serve some practical purpose or other, increase our possibilities or our efficiency.

Clothes, including hats, are necessary if we are to live in all the different parts of the world and go about in all sorts of weather. A chair enables one to adopt more attitudes than just those for which the body is built. The chair's back provides support for one's own back. A shelf on a wall is a tool for keeping things handy without having to cart them around the whole time. The most important of all our tools is the house – there is no end to what it does for us. To what extent churches or concert halls are to be reckoned as tools in the same practical sense is, of course, debatable, but even they protect those inside from the weather.

As long as these aids are thought of solely as tools they have usually been confined to essentials, that is to say their appearance has been formed by purely utilitarian considerations. But provided they are suitable for their purpose they will nonetheless be esteemed by those who are intimate with their use and dependent on them. Tools become an extension or an improved part of the user: a longer arm, a stronger hand.

It is his ability to make tools that has given man pre-eminence. As man has developed, he has made himself more and more dependent on tools. And *fondness for a good tool makes the user think it beautiful as well as useful.*

A good example of this is the ordinary axe. There is nothing about it that one could say was the result of personal taste or whim. As a whole, it is the sum of many experiences, all of them aimed at making it as serviceable as possible.

The beauty of the axe is that it is all governed by law: the relation of the length of haft to size and weight of blade, the interaction of its two materials, wood and steel – all seen against the background of people's experience of its efficiency. The next step brings us close to the basic rule governing everything that deserves to be called beautiful; that it must be distinguished by fitness for its purpose. The pointless, unserviceable things are ugly, an axehead on a broomstick for instance, or one that is irretrievably damaged.

The basis of this law can vary: axes with shorter or longer hafts or heads of different shapes than those of the first example need not necessarily be more ugly or better-looking. One will regard them as axes for different purposes, for chopping firewood, for felling trees or for finer carpenter's work, and still feel satisfied with them.

One cannot really say that an axe provides any great experience of beauty – it occupies too common-or-garden a place in our scheme of things, has too little excitement about it, for that. But a racing yacht or a fighter-plane is different. They too have had their shape determined largely by functional, fully comprehensible requirements, but the knowledge needed to satisfy these requirements is much more impressive. That is why the sight of these things can fill one with admiration and induce certain pleasurable, tingling sensations.

Good tools have their own clean beauty

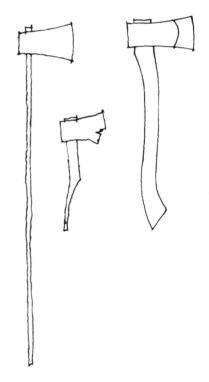

An axe is a good, well-designed tool
Ugly axes

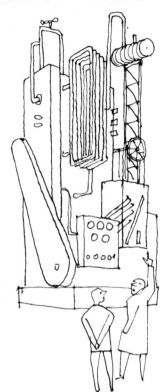

Functionally efficient =
beautiful?

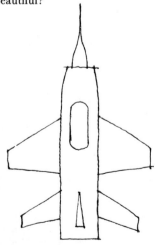

Supersonic jet fighter
Faster = more beautiful?

RESERVATION

Imagine visiting a factory and being shown a strange-looking machine. An engineer tells you enthusiastically that it is a perfect wonder, that it performs five operations simultaneously and in half the time that used to be required; but would you think the machine beautiful because of that? It is not at all certain that you would.

The difference is obvious enough: the axe, the yacht and the aeroplane have quite unambiguous functions: to chop wood, to move swiftly through the water with the help of the wind or through the air by burning paraffin. (Though if the aeroplane is a commercial model its function will be more complex, and the need for speed will have to be adapted to the requirement of providing a cabin that allows a certain number of passengers a reasonable degree of comfort.)

One has to understand a thing's function and what it is that makes it suited to its purpose, before one can see beauty in the functionally-shaped form. An axe can hardly arouse feelings of any depth in someone who has never held one in his hand. If that person nonetheless sees that it is well-shaped, that will be due to quite different causes. Our machine had nothing to say to us in this respect either.

Understanding of function does not always have to be based on personal experience or insight – very few people *know* what shape an aeroplane has to have in order best to fulfil its function. In such cases, one relies on other people's expert knowledge and allows it to fashion one's ideas. Yet at any time science can upset these ideas – when supersonic planes were first built they appeared to lack the qualities one had learned to esteem in their predecessors. It had transpired that the lean, aerodynamic lines of the latter were no longer suitable for the new, incredible speeds. This is another case of different shapes being needed in different circumstances, and one can still feel uncertain how far one will see a new shape as an independent expression of flight and speed.

No tool or anything else can have its shape determined solely and indisputably by functional considerations.

Manufacturing technique and its requirements also enter into it, and even when these requirements have been met, there will still be a greater or smaller amount of latitude allowing a choice of shape. Obviously, the more complicated a thing's function, the greater the possible choice will be. One will only be able to speak of a thing having inherent beauty when this possibility has been used further to emphasize the utility of the thing, the essential aspect of its function. Thus we have to do with feelings as well as knowledge – the situation has become more complex. And (we can assume) these feelings were not felt when the machine we were told was so wonderful was being designed.

Carving knives, all equally good
Function = form?

Let us go back to the sensible hat and take a closer look at it. It consists of a crown and a brim, the two elements that have always characterized the sensible hat. But the crown can be made low and close-fitting or it can be made higher. The latter can be defended on rational grounds, as it can only be good to have air between the top of the head and its protective covering. But how much higher the crown should be, is a matter for discussion.

The protective brim can be made so large that it acts as an umbrella, but it would then catch the wind and risk being blown off, and also it would require special arrangements to keep it stiff, for which reasons brims are usually much narrower. If the brim is quite flat it will still be difficult to keep it in shape without special stiffening. A conical shape would be the best way of ensuring that it was stiff enough in itself, but which way should it curve? If upwards, the brim would collect rain water, which can be an advantage, but only up to a certain point. It can be made to curve downwards so as *not* to collect water, but then the wearer must be prepared to get her shoulders wet. Or, if it is impossible to decide on either of the above courses, the brim can be turned down in front and up at the back. A certain amount of common sense comes into it, but in the last resort it will be a question of judgment, of what the wearer thinks looks best.

The particular hat we are talking about could be described as attractive in its honesty – at all events it is not

The *really* sensible hat?

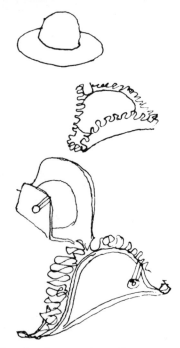

ugly. But its *effect* will vary depending on who is wearing it. If the head it is placed on looks that of an intellectual, somewhat sober type, one might consider that hat and head together comprise an unambiguous and thus confidence-inspiring whole. In another case it might provide a piquant contrast to a more frivolous face. In others again it might seem unsuitable and out-of-place.

Before leaving the subject of hats, let us recall the ingenuity that has been exercised over the centuries in varying the shape of hats. The three-cornered hat of the age of rococo, the Napoleon-style hat and the preposterous cocked-hat are all derived from ordinary hats with the brim turned up in different ways. People are not guided by common sense alone, yet what appears to be ingenuity run riot mostly started off as something familiar and unsophisticated, and this is especially true of clothes.

Starting from a quite ordinary hat . . .

CONSTRUCTION

What we have said so far concerning the relation between a thing's characteristics and common sense has all been connected with its *usability*.

But we also require that reason be employed in the way things are made. Whether your resources are money or your own hands and certain materials, the aim will always be to use them to the best advantage. In many cases, the fact that this has been done is difficult to establish from the mere appearance of the finished product; but at least it will be clearly expressed in everything to do with its *construction* – whether we are dealing with a bicycle frame, an old wooden or stone bridge or a modern one of steel or concrete.

One can safely say that the rule for what is desirable here is *that in meeting the requirements of constructional strength the least possible material shall be used.*

In the old days experience provided the only criterion; but to compensate for this the only materials used were

Suspension bridge
Functional = beautiful

those with whose performance everyone was more or less familiar and so everyone was in a position to appreciate elegance of construction. And people knew that the especially remarkable results had been achieved in the first place by painstaking attention to detail, whether this consisted in accurate dressing of the stone of the bold arch or of the joints in the parts of a wooden steeple.

Since the beginning of last century the dimensions of the joints in an exacting structure have been determined by exact calculation – that is to say they are of exactly the strength required by their place in the whole. This should mean that we could regard these calculated structures as perfect also in appearance. That this is far from being the case is owing to the fact that these calculations can never in themselves provide a basis for solving the task – they only come into it in the second stage. The first stage is the idea of how to set about things, in sketching something on which to base calculations; and this idea can be more or less good and imaginative. The use of more complicated methods of construction, especially when using ferro-concrete, has made it difficult for most people to understand the constructive principles employed and to have any direct sense of how the forces are distributed.

This aspect of the question provides an interesting example of how the concepts of ugly and good-looking can change, so to speak by resolution. Last century many of the typical constructions of the new age (cranes and that sort of thing) were thought to be condemned to ugliness, because their nature in no way corresponded with the rules for beauty on which the more traditional art of building was based.

After a bit, however, progressive-minded architects realized that it was ultimately untenable to regard a well-made tool as incompatible with what was held to be good-looking. And since it was not possible to change the nature of the crane, it was necessary somehow to arrive at a concept of architecture that was similarly characterized by the rational, for that was the only way in which cohesion could be restored to the total picture. Only by recognizing this rational architecture could one afford to build

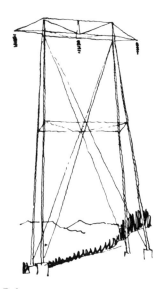

Pylon

Maximum of strength for the minimum of material

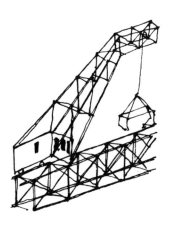

For a long time structures like this were incompatible with an ideal of architecture

15

The classical forms of capital:
Doric, Ionic and Corinthian, and
Romanesque

the dwellings and other structures which the growth of population and the new social situation required. One adopted an entirely new assessment of the ugly and the good-looking.

If you require that things be technically well made and in that sense good-looking, it also means that the materials used must correspond with the requirements of service-ability, and that the shaping of detail should conform to the distinctive qualities of these materials. Even in this age of plastics, the haft of an axe is still made of wood, because this is suitably springy and pleasant to handle. A tin capsule should preferably be curved, because quite flat surfaces bend more easily. And there is satisfaction in *understanding* this, just as there is in understanding a mathematical problem.

Our sense of the constructive finds satisfaction not only in appreciation of rational and finely balanced structures, but also in what provides expression of the constructive. A row of pillars is more expressive of support than a continuous wall, even though the wall can support a much greater load. It was this that induced the ancient Greeks to build their temples with pillars all the way round. In fashioning the individual pillars they displayed knowledge of the constructively expressive that has since been regarded as unsurpassable, especially where the capitals are concerned. Doric, Ionic and Corinthian capitals express, each in its own way, how the weight of the heavy beams is carefully transmitted to the slender neck of the pillar. The simple funnel-capital of the early Middle Ages is not as balanced in shape, nor as graceful, but it is convincing evidence of their understanding of construction.

ORDER AND DISORDER

The concept we call *order* and which in everyday life means an organized relationship between several things, also comes under the heading of the suitable and appropriate.

A desk piled higgledy piggledy with all sorts of things looks ugly – at least most people. This is not necessarily just the reaction of the strict, meticulous housewife. No reasonable person likes disorder, because disorder makes it impossible to register (or to find) what is actually there. When things are ordered and arranged, then everything is easy to see, systematized. *And it looks better.*

However, as the drawings show, order can be based on various principles that apply both to grouping the kinds of objects and placing these groups on the surface. In the second case one would soon become bewildered if one tried to use only reason; the basis will on the whole be different – what looks best and seems natural.

Anything that deserves to be called good-looking represents one form or another of order and organization.

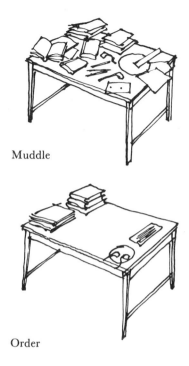

Muddle

Order

Mediaeval part of a town
Related forms, unschematic order

This applies both to the shaping of the individual objects and to their relationship one to another. It applies, for example, to the construction of a chair and to the chair's relationship with the rest of the furniture in the room, the relationship of the furniture to the room, the relationship of the room to the house, and the relationship of the house to the garden and landscape, or the town it is in.

The system of order adopted by an age or a milieu is the clearest indication of its state both materially and intellectually.

Experience

EXPERIENCE

All the indications of beauty we have mentioned so far have been the result of man's knowledge and experience, partly acquired directly and handed down from generation to generation, partly the result of new circumstances or come into existence in conjunction with new scientific knowledge. New situations can make it necessary to revise one's ideas of what is ugly and what is beautiful. But of course, we also have a lot of experience which has been accumulated over thousands of years and which lies so deep within us that we are no longer conscious of it – we are only aware of it if we note how we instinctively react to certain phenomena. This may be readily demonstrated by the various shapes of rooms.

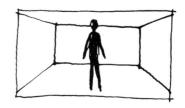

Uncomfortable

If a bird by mistake flies into your living room, it will flutter in panic from wall to wall with the feeling that it has been caught. And basically this is our human reaction too. We have learned to appreciate the shelter that walls and a roof provide, but at the same time they are a barrier, a confinement. We are more aware of this in certain circumstances than in others.

The room with a ceiling so low that one can scarcely stand upright in it can be made to seem cosy and sheltering by means of the right colours and furnishings. But without these it will seem oppressive. The same thing applies to a more or less windowless room with walls of rough stone, for rough walls seem more confining and repelling than smooth, even when we know that they are made of reinforced concrete and thus would actually be even more difficult to break through. A narrow, high-ceilinged room also arouses age-old primitive fears: it is as if we had fallen into a gorge and were unable to get out. There is a further example of this in the room with walls that twist and curve without the eye being able to discern any system or reason for their being like that or being able to see the area thus delimited. In such a room one has no orientation. An extreme form of this kind of room is the house of mysteries in amusement parks, which may also be equipped with mirrors and other things that add to one's bewilderment. There are exact medical terms for feelings of this kind:

uncomfortable

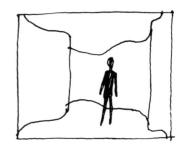

Uncomfortable
and again uncomfortable

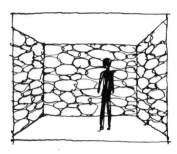

You wouldn't want to live here

Would you feel at home here?

Or here?

the panic caused by the feeling of being shut in is called claustrophobia; and the opposite, the feeling of being unprotected in exposed territory, is called agoraphobia.

The room in which one can feel at ease must provide the right mixture of openness and sheltering confinement. The solid protective factors are best neutralized by softer, more sympathetic elements. If, however, the latter get the upper hand, if windows and doors are surrounded by heavy draperies, the floor cluttered with over-upholstered chairs, the table with vases and candlesticks, that too will be wrong: you will feel that your freedom of movement is restricted and you will also feel a certain degree of discomfort owing to the fact that you cannot clearly register what you are actually seeing.

What cannot be registered, or put into some form of system, always appears disagreeable, that is to say: ugly. But when balancing the open against the sheltering, a variety of factors play a part and much depends on one's personal sense of security. The timid like to withdraw into a corner, and, indeed, in a restaurant, where we are among strangers, most of us prefer to sit against the wall or some other fixture.

A feeling as to security can set its stamp to a greater or lesser extent on a whole society – or generation. This may have been part of the reason why in the second half of the last century people liked to arrange their rooms in a way that today we regard as over-furnished. Although people were proud of the tremendous pace of development then, they were also rather scared by it – there was a great deal connected with it that they scarcely dared to face. But more of that later.

Everything man makes is intended to be used by people. In the case of railway bridges and suchlike, it is an indirect use, in so far as human measurements are not relevant, as they distinctly are in everything concerning houses.

There is, too, a direct connection between the human body and things, which we find in the units of measurements that all peoples originally used and which refer to various parts of the body: the small measurement was the breadth of a thumb, then the breadth of the hand (little used north of the Alps, but in Italy the old Roman *palma* was a common measure); then came the ell, which is the length from elbow to finger tips and after that the fathom, the spread of the arms. That most used after the inch, the breadth of the thumb, has been the *foot*.

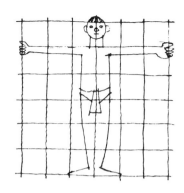

Foot and fathom

At an early stage of our development the individual used his own body to measure things by. Eventually people in one way or another agreed on units of fixed size which had a definite relationship one to another: the rule was twelve inches to the foot, two feet to the ell, and three ells to the fathom.

The Roman architect Vitruvius, who lived roughly at the same time as Julius Caesar and wrote the first book on architecture that we know of, explains many other relationships between the body and its limbs, which were obviously regarded as significant.

During the French revolution the old systems of measurement were replaced by the metre (supposed to be a ten millionth part of the length of a meridian from pole to equator) and this was divided according to the decimal system which makes calculation easier. This is now the standard system of measurement throughout Western Europe (not in the us, however; and in the UK it will not be officially adopted until 1975). The metric system lacks that immediate, intimate connection with human measurements. However, people will always use their experience of the body's needs in judging the suitability of dimensions.

When everything in a room is attuned to the measurements of the body, the whole is in harmony. Even though

Higher doorway = greater dignity?

21

it seems obvious that this is what should happen, there have been times – including today – when we have let other considerations play a part. For example, in Renaissance palaces the height of the door was made to depend on the dimensions of the wall area, and in the last century or so similarly unreasonably high doors were built in ordinary houses to provide a pompous frame for those entering through them. Our modern sober-minded age considers that a person's importance should be measurable by other and more reliable means. Nonetheless, in contemporary homes you will often find armchairs that seem to have been made for elephants rather than for humans, while the coffee cups displayed on the dresser are almost doll's house size.

Some time ago, as a reaction against the pretentiousness of the past, it became the fashion to make everything as low as possible. It was almost impossible to get out of the chairs and you had to go down on your knees to find a book even on the top shelf of the bookcase. It is not easy to practise moderation. Even the most sensible people still refuse to buy beds the height of those in hospitals, despite the fact that these are the easiest to make and to get into and out of.

Take that excellent expression 'elbow room'. This does not imply that we want to jostle and hit out with our elbows, but that we need to feel that there is the *space* to do so. This is one of the body's natural rights, and one that is very often neglected in furnishings and arrangements. We need to be able to stretch out our arms, keep people and things at arm's length. If you mark off the length of your arm on the wall with a piece of chalk, you may be surprised how long it is. We also feel a need to be able to *walk about,* even indoors, to be able to take a sufficient number of steps for the body to be in relaxed, natural movement.

Chairs occupy a special position among the articles of furniture whose shape is intimately linked to that of the body and its needs. The function of the chair is so important that one would expect it to have been fully researched and a more or less ideal shape arrived at very early on, but this is far from being the case. Most people today would say that the elegant chairs of the end of the seventeenth century are horrible to sit on. The seat is both too shallow and too high, the back too narrow, straight and steep; you feel almost pushed forward by it.

This is not to say that the furniture makers of those days lacked the necessary insight and that the more comfortable chairs we go in for today are the result of some later discovery – like the invention of the steam engine. The truth is that no one then felt any need for a different kind of chair – they liked to sit in that way. But then they had other needs and a different attitude to life altogether.

Modern ideas have led doctors to investigate carefully what positions are best for our spines, yet still only a few of the chair-designs on the market are based on their findings – most are based on less practical ideas of the functions a chair has to fulfill.

Intended to impress

Was this chair made for people or for elephants?

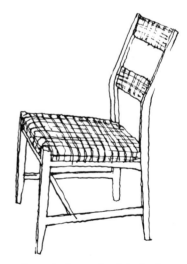

and to suit the needs of the body

23

Hat

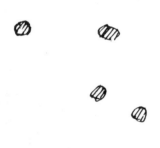

experiment

There is no need at this stage to describe the hat we are discussing: just look at the drawing.

Now let us try a little experiment. It may seem exaggeratedly simple, but you will find that it is of significance. You take four pebbles, balls of paper or something similar and drop them on the table. That's all.

One result could be that shown in the drawing, that is to say that the pebbles are lying in a way that to the sensitive eye of the artist might seem an interesting combination, but which to most people will seem to be what it is, purely fortuitous: something formless, something with no explicable or memorable connection, more or less as good as nothing. To many people it will be even worse, something irrelevant and embarrassing, only fit for the waste paper basket.

Now imagine yourself leaving the room and returning to find that someone has moved the pebbles and arranged them as in the second drawing. The first thing we shall see is that the new arrangement is not the work of playful kittens – *only a human being could have done it in that way.* The whole thing is still just nonsense, it still has no obvious purpose and amounts to nothing. But nonetheless it is something now, something definite that exists on its own, in its abstract value. (Abstract just means seen for itself, without links to other values or qualities.)

This something is a *square*. This means that the points mark a regular figure, a quadrilateral the four sides of which are of equal length with the angles between them of equal size, in this case ninety degrees, thus right angles. By these simple means we have thus established the highest conceivable degree of order – an order that can also be characterized as *form*, and that can both be remembered and described exactly.

The previous chapter should have made it clear that if a thing is to be described as good-looking, order, in the practical sense, is a prerequisite. The same criterion can be applied on the abstract plane.

Is this square, then, really a good-looking figure? Yes, it is. We could even call it divine, say that it represents an incontrovertible and universal truth, since a square was a square to the ancient Egyptians as it is to us and as it will continue to be here or on Mars for all eternity. No new experience can change that. And to what is universal one must bow respectfully and find it beautiful.

On the other hand no one will go into ecstasies at the sight of this figure, but that is only because it is so basic in its nature and something that we are accustomed to reckon by and base our registration on. Today and in the past architects have delighted in building houses with square ground plans, because they felt that this made the point of departure absolute and incontestable.

When a figure that is *nearly* a square can seem so interesting, it is because our ability to judge is being tested. Are we wrong, or are two of the sides really longer than the other two? Or, if we are in no doubt about this, what is the reason for the disparity? A question has been introduced, something that can be deliberately used to produce the feeling of something more exciting or inciting.

Apart from the square, the main elementary, regular figures are the circle and the equilateral triangle. Regular pentagons and hexagons can also be included, but as the number of sides increases, the strikingness of the figure is reduced. As well as their regularity all these figures have this in common, that they appear static – which means they seem to be at rest, sufficient unto themselves. Otherwise, they are obviously different in character and this we shall come back to later.

Corresponding to the two-dimensional figures that one can draw on a flat surface are a number of three-dimensional ones representing volume. The cube consists of six square surfaces. Four equilateral triangles can be put together to form a triangular pyramid, while the apotheosis of the circle is the sphere, which has no flat surfaces, just a continuous curve that is exactly the same everywhere. These again represent what is eternally valid, the

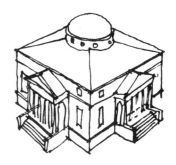

Square house built by Palladio about 1550

Near-squares

25

A cube

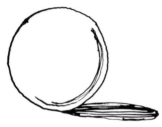

A sphere

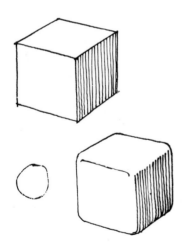

Top: an *exact* cube. *Below:* the same cube with rounded edges making it look *heavier*.

absolute, and thereby form a basis for all appreciation of form.

The cylinder, the rectangular pyramid and the cone also have a certain fundamental character, but are not so absolute, since the relation between the base and the height can be varied without the figures losing their right to their name.

This is the moment to go back to our hat and find that its shape can be clearly described in one single word, namely *cone.* If you add to that the word *low,* you have described still more and if you give measurements of its breadth and height, you have a mathematically accurate description. Its most marked characteristics must lie here, in the fact that it is of a definite *shape.* In addition there is the special relationship between its shape and the face beneath it.

You cannot possibly say that a sphere is more or less handsome than a cube – to do so would be setting up in judgment over the universe. The sphere and the cube have different characteristics that can be more or less appropriate in different connections.

We might say that one of them appears soft, the other hard. We are here applying our practical experience to these shapes even in connections where there is no question of making practical use of them. Their abstract qualities are extended by means of *associations.*

The cube is described as hard because it has sharp edges which look potentially hurtful. It also appears hard because one imagines that it will have to be made of a relatively hard material in order to retain its sharp-edged shape. The sphere, on the other hand, could be a lump of clay rolled into a ball or made of rubber. And even if it is made of stone, the risk of hurting oneself on it is slight.

Conversely, the cube appears light because its finely polished form could equally well be made up of thin plates – it does not give any real impression of mass. If, however, you make it actually lighter by grinding away the edges and rounding them, it will *look* heavier because it then gives a greater impression of massiveness. The sphere looks much more integrated and therefore heavier.

One begins to understand that anyone who forms things in his hands has ways of deliberately inducing certain reactions in people looking at what he has made – if their eyes are open. A thing that is to give the impression of being good to handle should have soft lines. If it is to seem friendly, the soft must be combined with the light. To convey a sense of seriousness and solidity, one must use heavy and perhaps hard lines.

In certain cases, abstract forms can have another, quite different quality. Take for example the cone.

Cones run up into a point and express themselves in a way different from either the sphere or the cube – especially in their more slender forms there is something stabbing about them. But something else, too.

As we have said, the cone is not fixed in shape – the relation between height and diameter of base can be varied, making the cone look tall or low. One should also be able to make it look neither the one or the other, and it would be reasonable to suppose that the relationship necessary to achieve this effect could be geometrically worked out. There would seem to be two possibilities here: either to make the height and the diameter of the base equal – as if the cone had been cut from a cube – or to let the diameter correspond to the distance from the top to the foot measured along the outside in such a way that the section would be an equilateral triangle. But you will see that both these cones look tall, more so of course in the case of the former.

In both cases the cone will clearly seem to be pointing upwards; it will induce an upward movement in the eye and thereby also give the impression of being itself in a sort of motion in the same direction, But if it is made low, it will look as if it were sliding downwards and outwards.

To arrive at the cone that appears neither high nor low, that does not suggest movement in any direction, one has to rely on one's eye. The normal cone is not geometrically determined and thus it is difficult to say anything about its measurable qualities, but most people will get the impression of stillness from a cone with an angle of about fifty-three degrees between base and sides (as opposed to

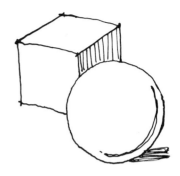

The sphere is *soft* and *firm;* the cube *hard* and angular.

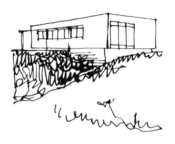

Light house of concrete (clean surfaces and corners) and heavy timber house (rough surfaces, blurred corners)

A *cone* thrusting upwards

and another sagging downwards

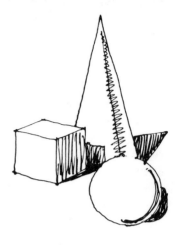

A little drama in 3 acts

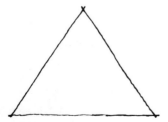

Equilateral triangle –
upward movement
Static?

The upward-striving
and that which leans heavily
on the ground

the sixty degrees of the equilateral triangle). The Egyptian pyramids have this angle and they certainly look absolutely static. But as we are now talking of pyramids, not cones, things will differ, depending on whether one looks at them from the front, so that only one side is visible, or diagonally when it is the angle not of the side-surface but of the side-edges that provide the outline.

One can take a cube, a sphere and a cone and place them together, thereby composing a little drama in three acts. A person with experience can place the forms together in such a way that the beholder's eye is forced to follow them in a planned order, providing a course of action.

What gives the impression of movement is an important aid to the architect, but it can very easily lead the inexperienced astray. It seems meaningful when the tall spire on a church keeps pointing heavenwards, or when its low squat roof makes the mountain hut seem to be crouching down on the ground. In neither case can the motion seem disquieting, since no one can doubt that gravity will keep the church from taking off, or that the solidity of the ground will stand up to the pressure exerted by the shape of the roof.

It is different when the feeling given is of movement slantwise or horizontal, since there is nothing to restrain it, unless something is shaped to pull in the opposite direction. It is a basic need of us all that our surroundings should provide mental rest and peace, all that is but those things that have motion as their object.

That the arm of a signpost continues pointing is reasonable, even though we want it to stay where it is. But pictures hung along a slanting line point in a way that is meaningless, as if they were trying to attract attention to a point in the ceiling or something going on in the cellar. If the pictures are hung level, along a horizontal line but only in one half of the wall area, they can seem to be trying to escape out of the house.

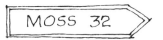

No doubt of the direction of the town of Moss

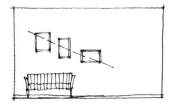

Unrestful = ugly way of hanging pictures

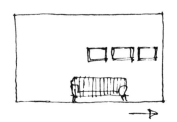

The sprouting plant fills us with wonder

This chapter could have started with a description of the second of the two good-looking hats, if only it had been possible to describe it. One could call it crumpled and peculiar, but there one would stick as far as words go and that would scarcely be adequate to give anyone even an approximately satisfying picture of the phenomenon. So here, too, we must be content with a drawing.

As our intelligent student has thought the hat worth her notice, we must assume that *its* qualities also represent a kind of order and system. And, strange as it may sound when applied to such an artificial, extravagant, even silly, creation, I will maintain that there is something *natural* about it.

We are said to be living in a technological world, surrounded as we are by refrigerators, vacuum cleaners, electric lamps and television sets technically so complicated that most of us cannot begin to understand them. Add to these our buses, trains, motor cars and aeroplanes. Although our surroundings are not entirely mechanical, they will mostly be the work of human hands. For a great many people Nature is something only seen on Sundays.

Man is said to have lived on earth for some 600,000 years but of this time we have been more or less conscious of ourselves for only 6–7000 years. Of this period the so-called technological age accounts for no more than 200 at the most. We are not born with an instinct for washing-machines, but the essence of *Nature* is implanted in us, is part of our equipment. And no experiences of our surroundings affect us more deeply than those that concern the products of Nature.

As children, most of us have played with sea shells and snail shells, fir-cones and shiny brown conkers which we have held in our hands for the sheer pleasure of feeling them, we may have picked flowers and cut branches and twigs. All this forms a firm foundation for our being able to register the essence of things. Above all, we are ourselves the product of Nature.

Everything in Nature is lovely. That, of course, is just an opinion; it cannot be proved. But all products of Nature can be called beautiful, simply because we cannot imagine how else they should be and because it is quite pointless to criticize them and also because we are incapable of making anything like them.

You may well protest against the assertion that everything in Nature is lovely, saying that toads, perhaps, or snakes, are terrifying and repulsive. They may be – to you.

This is something that occurs in many contexts. A thing can be lovely in the absolute, objective sense – seen with unbiased eyes – and at the same time *not* appear so when seen from a subjective, personally coloured point of view. When we think certain of the creations of Nature unattractive in appearance, this is not because they are ugly, but because they fill us with fear, because their appearance or their slimy skin is incompatible with our own interests, or because they were created for life under conditions alien to human beings. Life in mud puddles and ponds is not for us.

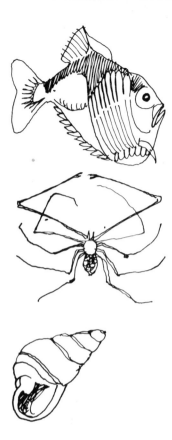

Conversely, it is reasonable that we should find special beauty in the creatures that impress us by their size, strength, agility or swiftness, because they have qualities that we envy. Yet even though many animals surpass humans in one or more of these fields, we allow ourselves to regard our own bodies as the most glorious of all Nature's products, though we may not admit it.

But it is one thing to delight in the multiplicity of examples that Nature holds up before us and quite another to make use of them. The artificial flower is and remains artificial, and the more closely it resembles what it is copying, so that perhaps you have to touch it before you discover that it is artificial, the more disagreeable we think the deception. It is a cheat. We have meddled with something we have no right to touch and we do not have the ability even approximately to give it the one essential, life.

What one must ask of the works of man is something

All Nature's forms are made with care and precision

quite different: namely that they shall be what they are, that in their greater or lesser degree of perfection they shall be manifestations of human skill, thought and emotion. Again, our experience of our own products lies on quite a different plane from our experience of Nature. In the case of Nature it is more a question of uncomplicated enjoyment, a kind of pleasurable ascertaining of facts. Where man-made things are concerned our feelings are more complex, because they give us a sort of picture of our inner being and so require that we adopt an attitude towards them.

To benefit from the teaching of Nature one has to try to *translate* it. The first thing that comes to mind in this connection is the concept of character.

To us the lines of the stag symbolize all that is fitting and graceful

The eagle is the king of birds

CHARACTER

Anyone asked what this drawing represented would un-hesitatingly answer: *a tree*. And they would do so, despite the fact that we can most certainly assume that there is nowhere on God's green earth a tree that looks just like that. This is a situation the diametrical opposite to that of the square. The square is a *hypothetical* concept and no drawing can depict a square without actually being one. Our drawing of a tree is not a tree, just a drawing; how-ever one can safely say that it represents or has the *character* of a tree.

What do you think this is?

Like the four pebbles dropped on to the table top, it is a figure that is stamped by the fortuitous, that is very nearly just a scribble. Shut the book and you will not be able to describe it or copy it exactly. But everyone will be able to make a different drawing that to the same degree has the character of a tree. Thus there must be something that distinguishes it – in this case a certain consistency in the way the lines are combined to make trunk, branches and twigs.

Obviously, there can be nuances in this consistency. Look at the next two drawings: in principle these are the same as the first, yet one has the character of an oak and the other of an ash. Each is stamped by its own kind of order, which cannot be registered by means of practical experience or knowledge of geometry, but which is dis-tinguished in a kinship between the individual parts. This kind of order is often called organic, from *organum* meaning a living unit.

An oak

We have it in our power to break this consistent form of order – on paper. You can draw a palm-tree with a couple of pine-branches. If the intention was to be facetious the result may well be successful. Even someone who has never seen either a palm-tree or a fir will see that the draw-ing was meant to be funny, something impossible.

There is nothing to stop a joiner making a table with four legs, two of steel tubing and two of carved mahogany; but it will look meaningless, to the point of being repulsive.

These are rather crude and more or less inconceivable examples of how we react to self-made things on the basis

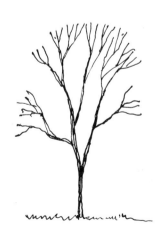

and an ash

33

and a palm-tree
with pine-branches

of knowledge drawn from Nature. You can also say that it is contrary to common sense to make a table like that. It would be more convincing if you could illustrate the point on the abstract plane and show that organic cohesion is needed there too.

To do this I have drawn what is just a wavy line. There is support for saying that it has organic character in the fact that the hand that drew it was impelled in the same supple, easy movements the whole way.

Rub out part of this line and replace it with a jerky, angular piece made with quite different movements of the hand, and the kinship between the parts will have been lost. The line now looks disjointed, inorganic, ugly.

If you take a really well-shaped chair from the days of rococo and saw it up, the pieces will still have things in common. Things made at that time provide particularly good examples of this. A chair with steel legs and uphol-stered seat and back does not seem to satisfy the require-ment of organic consistency nearly as well. On the con-trary, here the emphasis is on the contrast between the parts which are different in principle, the easy and com-fortable and those that just support. The appeal here in the first place is to the law of the functional and the con-structive. But thereby it can also be made to look organic, as a man-made thing, though in a more indirect sense.

And to return for a moment to Nature, it should be remembered that natural order is not only found in live and growing things – it is also found in the wind playing with the desert sand or the waves striking on the bottom in shallow water. Patterns are formed where you can never distinguish two exactly similar parts, yet at the same time the overall formation is of uniform character.

And in crystals Nature and man's ability to think up independent geometric abstractions meet.

34

MODULE AND PROPORTIONS

All the leaves on a tree are roughly of the same size, and just as big on a young tree as on one of the same kind that has reached maturity. Apart from the fact that this adds to the impression of it being an organic whole, it also enables one better to assess the difference in size, since there is this common basis for comparison. Similarly, a child's head early on is all but full size, so that the relation between head and body gives a clear indication of a person's height even in a picture.

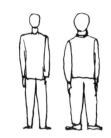

Are these two equally tall?

The architect uses the same method in order to maintain his scale. If in one façade you place two windows with the same division into panes and the same proportions of height and width, but of different size, the effect is confusing. The smaller window looks like a stunted version of the larger, or as if it belonged to a smaller house, or was in a different, more distant plane.

People very early paid attention to this need to provide the effect of a harmonious whole; particularly perhaps in the rules the ancient Greeks set up for building their temples, the dimensions and proportions of which were the product of one and the same basic measurement, the same *module*. This module was usually the diameter of the column at its base. Once this had been decided all the other measurements followed from it, however big or small the temple was to be. The same comfortable sense of order and organic cohesion is given by the even spaces between the uprights in old half-timbered houses, even though here the point of departure was ordinary common sense.

It looks as if these windows were in different planes . . .

It was the Greeks, too, who were the first to philosophize on the essence of beauty and they soon came to the conclusion, often advanced, that here too there must be an inner rule of law, of the kind valid in geometry and in Nature, with the human body as the point of departure. The individual parts of the structure should go together as naturally as fingers, hand, lower- and upper-arm join together. And, as already mentioned, the aim was to achieve a proportional order of magnitudes, the *proportions* which seemed harmonious. One theory launched by Pythagoras was that the proportion between the lengths of

. . . just as these men are at different distances

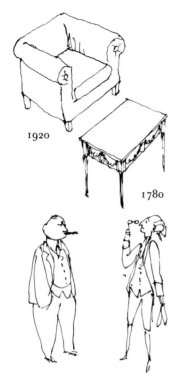

1920

1780

Unfortunate juxtaposition of forms and dimensions

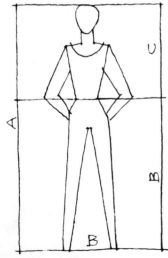

The golden section

the strings of a harp which provides the harmony for the ear, also appears harmonious to the eye.

It is not possible to determine in an absolute sense to what degree these propositions are valid. It depends on what one is aiming at. The beauty one can find in a tree is, of course, not stamped by such conditions. But when looking at the human figure, we are very particular in our ideas of what is well-formed.

Certain proportions keep recurring in the representative architecture of the various historical periods, even if it is difficult to demonstrate to what degree architects have been conscious of using them. These are the proportions that are basically those of the human body.

If you draw a horizontal line dividing the human body at the waist, this gives three measurements: the full height of the body, A; the height from the soles of the feet to the navel, B; and from the navel to the crown of the head, C. Their relationship one to another has a definite, although in practice of course rarely exact, correspondence: the whole height is to the greater part, as the greater part is to the lesser. It can also be phrased in this way, that the greater part is the mean proportional between the whole and the lesser part, as expressed as a formula, thus:

Assuming that $A = B + C$, $A : B = B : C$.

The effect of this proportion can be seen if you make a rectangle the sides of which correspond to A and B or, if you like, to B and C. Such a rectangle looks neither particularly high nor low, but just right. Even if this does not appear immediately obvious, as in the case of the square, you will quickly see how its character changes the moment you try to alter it.

This is the proportion of the golden section, which has enjoyed varying acceptance and which has also played a part in modern architecture, for the great Corbusier swore by it, or rather the series of proportions that can be derived from it.

All living creatures are built symmetrically, that is to say they consist of exactly similar halves placed together but with one reversed mirror-wise. (The only exceptions are

36

fish of the flounder family, which special conditions have made lopsided.) It has always seemed correspondingly desirable to make houses and the great majority of things of everyday use in accordance with this principle. It is only recently that architects have dared deliberately to flout it – and in the Middle Ages it was not taken so seriously.

But what about our hat and its connection with what we have been saying? It does not appear to apply the golden section and it is not symmetrical. Nor is it like either a flower or an animal. If it nonetheless has a connection, this must be because its essence is organic in character, a to-some-extent-natural product of the qualities of its material, felt, and its composition, supported by an inner connection between all its parts, akin to that you find in anything that grows. If you take a closer look at it, perhaps it is a bit like a mushroom?

Symmetrical façade 1700s

Asymmetrical façade 1945

Chapter Five

THE ORDER IN RHYTHM, BALANCE AND GROUPING

The three systems of order

Let us briefly recapitulate the observations made so far, before we start trying to explain the more complex phenomena involved in numbers.

We have seen that if things are to look seemly, either individually or collectively, some sort of order must prevail in them. In principle, this order can be divided into three groups; serviceability and fitness (the axe); shape or formal arrangement (the cube); and the organic (the tree). But beauty is not necessarily the immediate result of order being established. You can truly say that a classroom with the desks arranged in straight lines and rows has been ordered, but there is no guarantee at all that you will feel comfortable there. It would be safer to say that a thing must be well-ordered before it can be attractive or good-looking.

We have further seen that the different kinds of order call forth different reactions. Where the appearance of an object in the first place tells of its use, we will derive from it feelings associated with our own experience and knowledge. These can be pleasurable, characterized by familiarity with the object, unpleasant, or even feelings of horror. A guillotine is not an object you can consider as an abstract form, without thinking of its function. On the other hand, with the sphere and the cube one's reaction is purely to the abstract quality of geometrically determined order, because the two forms are what they are and nothing else.

The most difficult to define is organic order. It is to be found in innumerable versions, and you sense it rather than are able to demonstrate it. In Nature it is bound up with a corresponding multiplicity of expressions – you can speak of a fir being proud, an oak powerful, a spruce or weeping willow sad. Flowers have even more to tell, even though gentleness figures in most. None of these attributed qualities have anything to do with reality; in every case we are just expressing our reaction to their shape and lines.

The strongest associations, however, would seem to be those linked to living creatures, headed by man himself. If we can speak of strokes on a piece of paper as being supple, slack, brutal, graceful and energetic, it is in the first place because we are using our own experience of corresponding attitudes in people.

In everyday life it is, of course, rare to come across things whose form of order is based on only one of these three categories – as a rule they are all three together. Most chairs provide good examples of this combination, you cannot see a chair without mentally sitting in it, trying it out, and you may even do so in actual fact. And even when it is made of thin pieces with large gaps between them, the eye will take it in as a closed form. Its organic form is to be found in the relationship between the dimensions of its parts and the materials, and in the way in which they are put together.

Though it may seem that the artist has plenty of effects at his disposal, we have still not mentioned all of them.

A straight line is a quite definite concept. It indicates the shortest distance between two points. This is a strict definition – the line cannot have the least bend without its being noticeable as a fault. And so the straight line is itself regarded as severe. On the other hand a line drawn with a light, playful hand without thought of definitions will be correspondingly playful, even gay and abandoned. Or it can be drawn with angular movements and so become itself angular and unapproachable. These effects can be strengthened by repetition, thus producing that peculiar phenomenon called rhythm.

Chair with *closed* shape, Renaissance

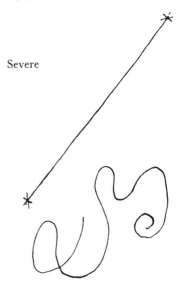

Severe

and gay

RHYTHM

The beating heart, the even breathing of a sleeping child, those thrilling indications of life, are mysteriously fascinating. So is everything that is continually repeated, whether it is relatively regular like waves breaking over a rock, or more irregular like the leaping flames of a bonfire. The mystery of rhythm is especially pronounced when it is in the form of sound – the drum is probably the oldest of all instruments – but it can also be conveyed without sound, using line and shape.

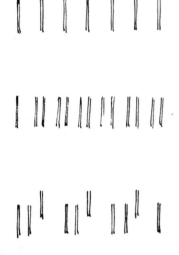

It is difficult to put into words what is the actual import of the different rhythms of form. But if you make a few short strokes at equal intervals, at least you can see that this has produced a rhythm, as calm and regular as the tread of a sentry. You can put the strokes together in pairs and at once the whole thing has become more exciting, as if the larger gaps created a sort of expectation. Or you can arrange them in threes with the third protruding a little above the other two. This introduces two-directional movement, making the rhythm more jerky or gayer, as if it too was taking joyous hops. But in every case the decisive thing is that the concept of *time* somehow or other seems to have entered into the picture – you *follow* the rhythm, are carried along on its even or leaping course. You are in its power.

To take examples from other spheres. Everyone will appreciate that the waltz is quite different from the tango and will invoke an essentially different feeling. It is possible to explain the exact differences in the sequence of short and long steps, but more difficult to say where the differences in feeling arise. These rhythms can be drawn,

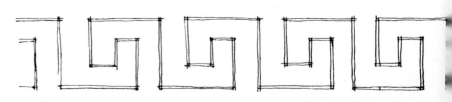

Rhythm in ornament

though I do not suppose everyone will find my attempts satisfactory. This is such a many-sided subject that everyone will have his own idea of it.

The concept of rhythm can manifest itself in all sorts of sequences, and not just as a repetition of dots and lines. The module-principle that we have already mentioned will also give a sense of there being a rhythmic relationship, provided the module appears in accordance with a system so that the eye can follow its course throughout the composition. In many buildings the window-rhythm is the most characteristic element.

Otherwise rhythm is best known in connection with pattern or ornament, the essence of which is repetition, and which is often used to link surfaces and lines to something which can be clearly registered, something on which you want the eye to rest.

Rhythm: sound and movement

Waltz and tango

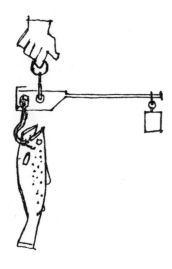

Scales and steelyard

The safe feeling of balance between forms is based partly on experience and partly on purely abstract conditions of visual character.

As we know, in practice balance can be achieved in two ways. One is to put bodies of equal weight at the end of lever-arms of equal length such as you get in a pair of scales. This kind of balance provides a more or less symmetrical image. The other way is allow a heavier object at the end of a short arm to be counter-balanced by a lighter object – the weight – at the end of a longer arm. This is the principle of the steelyard, which provides an asymmetrical image.

Our experience in this field can lead us to ask for similar versions of balance in the interplay of forms, if we are to be able to call the result static in the visual sense. But, of course, these systems cannot be transferred directly – in practice the *sight* of the weights and things to be weighed does not give a clear feeling of weight. A bag full of feathers and a bag full of shot can look exactly the same. Here again it is a question of feelings, yet here most people's reactions will be the same or similar as soon as they become aware of the relationship.

Within a limited, regular surface, the point of balance will be spontaneously taken as lying on the vertical centre-line of the surface. Windows in similar positions in either half of a façade give a feeling of balance. One large window near the centre-line can be balanced by a smaller one, at a greater distance on the other side, on the principle of the steelyard. But, strangely enough, a single window, placed up in one corner of an otherwise blank wall, can do the same. This is because the wall is not made of air – you are letting the pronouncedly dark shape of the window be balanced by the actual mass of the wall-surface.

A group of furniture placed in a corner can give the impression that the whole room is on the point of tilting over. If the furniture is arranged symmetrically against the wall, you will achieve the requisite sense of rest – perhaps to excess, to the point of boredom, some may say.

A balance that is symmetrical will combine rest with a degree of excitement which will call for greater thought to establish, or about which you will not feel sure until you have been able to assess the position more accurately.

The requirement of order, about which we are always speaking, can also be said to represent an urge to *unite*. This urge is so deep-rooted that the eye will start doing this on its own in an attempt to create some sort of order even in a situation of chaos. This can be seen in connection with the concept called the *group*.

Strangely enough there is balance here too

The firmament is chaotic. There is no demonstrable organization or system in the confusion. But that is more than the eye can come to terms with. It selects those stars that are especially bright and draws invisible lines between them, turning them into groups – figures that the mind can retain. Not only that, but with a considerable amount of imagination one can draw lines *round* these figures, making them resemble familiar things: a pair of scales, a plough, a bear, a scorpion or a man, Orion. In all ages men have seen these same shapes in the stars, although their ideas as to what they represent has varied a bit.

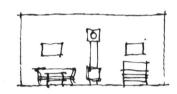

This certainly balances

Back on earth, we can resume our experiments with the four stones which we had arranged to form a square. Note that we said to form or represent, because of course they were not a square – just four points. But the eye joins them into a group, drawing lines from point to point in the *shortest way*.

If we now move these points closer and closer together, still retaining the right angles, we will in the first place go on thinking we see a rectangle, but one that is smaller and more oblong-extended. At a certain stage, however, this impression will disappear and from being a group the four points will become two groups of only two stones each. If they still indicate anything, it will be two short lines, independent of each other. And this despite the fact that none of the distances has been increased. What has happened is that the fields of force of the points have changed with the new constellation.

This tilts

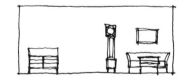

This balances

Still one group

but now there are *two* groups

The eye's liking to have things presented in distinct groups is very strong. The most obvious example of this is the arrangement of furniture in an ordinary living-room. If the sofa, chairs, table, etc. are placed about the floor at equal intervals, the eye will wander round helplessly as it attempts to find a resting place. But if you arrange the furniture in groups: the sofa, coffee-table and two arm-chairs in one group, dining-table and chairs in another, work things in another, the eye will find rest on each and be saved the effort of trying itself to establish a system. This grouping can with advantage be emphasized with rugs or carpets, pictures on the walls and other cohesive effects. In fact the appearance of the individual objects, that is whether they are ugly or good-looking, seems to be less important than the way in which they are arranged. But it must be admitted that contemporary designers and archi-tects prefer the less regular, more exciting forms of group-order and balance, and this makes it difficult for others to keep pace. In the days when the living-room was arranged symmetrically with the table in the middle of the floor, providing a fixed point of departure, anybody at all could see the intended pattern.

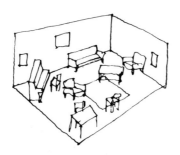

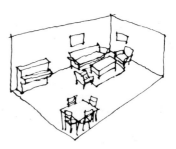

We like to have things arranged in groups

Similarly, the basis of our assessment of what is right and wrong in the world of shapes, especially where buildings and their furnishings are concerned, is based on definite fundamental knowledge. We *know* that a stretch of water is horizontal, and that a line with a weight at the end of it hangs vertically; and also that the angle between these two is a right angle. Though in the world of aesthetics a great deal is relative, one can without hesitation state that when a picture is hung awry it is ugly.

All knowledge helps us to understand what we see – even this. When reinforced concrete was new and first made it possible to construct things that seemingly defied the laws of gravity, it was natural that people took a triumphant delight in using it in that way. A typical example is the diving-tower that leans out over the water. Once this had been demonstrated a few times, however, it was no longer so amusing. In Pisa there is a particularly lovely tower that has become ugly because subsidence of the ground has made it lean over. It was built intended to be vertical, as are all proper towers.

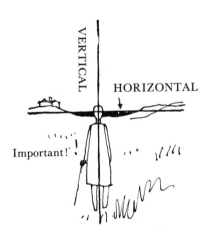

Chapter Six

HOW FORM IS INFLUENCED BY COLOUR,
BY THE CHARACTER OF SURFACES AND
BY LIGHT

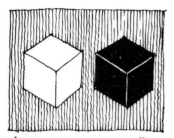

larger   smaller
(light)   (heavy)

Still heavier

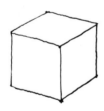

Colour the top and one side red

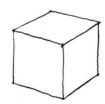

Paint the whole red

One of our women's hats was red, so red that the most characteristic thing about it was its redness; it was a red hat. The colour was so dominant that it had become the dominant feature and more important than the shape.

Colour is too complex a thing to go into in a book of this length. Here we must be content with a schematic demonstration of how it affects shape.

To begin with, let us confine ourselves to black and white and use two cubes for our demonstration. The way the eye and the optical nerves are arranged, the white cube appears to be larger than the black, although they are exactly equal. And since we all the time have a suspicion that this may be the case, the one that appears the larger, must at the same time appear to have a smaller specific weight, that is: to be lighter. White makes things appear light and airy; black makes them look heavy and concentrated.

Combining this with what we already know of heavy/ light effects, we can use light or dark colours to emphasize the impressions of lightness and heaviness given by other things.

Obviously, the right thing is to get effects of shape and light to work together towards a common end. However, one can imagine occasions when one wishes to reduce an unavoidable, obtrusive effect of shape by using colour. It will demonstrate the possibilities of this if we use crayons on these cubes without for the moment worrying about what is right and wrong.

Colour the top and one side of the first cube red, leaving the other side white, and imagine that the opposite side is white too; the other two sides being red. This will at once considerably reduce the cube's character as a homogeneous, independent unit. Rather it will now seem to be a piece cut off a much longer bar which is red outside and white inside.

With the second cube, colour each of the visible sides a different colour: one yellow, one green and one red. This will give an even more confusing effect – and the appearance of massiveness, in particular, will have gone. Yet another cube can be coloured in stripes and blobs, causing complete confusion. In practice, of course, one does this only when the intention *is* to confuse, to make a thing invisible by disrupting its shape. This is one aspect of *camouflage;* animals use it constantly, man uses it in war.

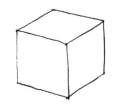

Use yellow, red and green, one colour to each side

The lessons to be learned from these experiments are fairly obvious: to paint the outside of a house with different colours on each wall – as some people unfortunately are tempted to do – is just ugly. A house should look secure and fixed, be a whole, be a *house.* And wall should be wall all the way round it. (It is another matter if the materials are different in the bearing and non-bearing walls. The difference there has a meaning.)

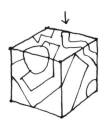

Use different colours for the figures and the form of the cube will be reduced

Things are not quite the same in the case of a room. Rooms are made up of three different elements: a solid floor, protective walls and a covering ceiling. If all of these have the same colour or are made of the same

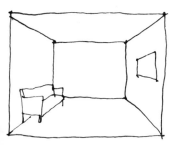
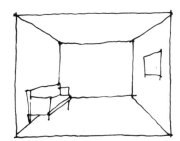
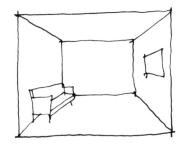

Paint the walls and ceilings with different colours and see how the character of the room changes

material, it can be oppressive and look as if the room were not built of surfaces, but hollowed out of a compact mass. It seems natural to allow the parts to have individuality. As a rule one lets the ceiling be the lightest in colour, in that way giving the room an airy, unoppressive appearance. But if the room seems disturbingly high, so that you get that feeling of being in a ravine, this sensation can be reduced by making the ceiling the darker part.

On occasion it can be an advantage to make one wall a different colour from the others, thereby emphasizing that a room is a union of surfaces, and this also makes the whole lighter and less enclosing. If this is to be done successfully, you have to take into consideration how the light falls in through the windows, the shape of the room and the arrangement of the furniture.

Monochrome materials against walls of another plain colour make everything stand out clearly. The effect can be made softer by using carpets and textiles with patterns of multiple colours, but if the pattern is too violent or garish, it will mess up the shapes unpleasantly to the extent of camouflaging them. Here, as in all other spheres, uncertainty is a bad thing.

Here the different elements are clearly stated

The same room and restless patterns have effaced the image

The simple colours found in the spectrum of sunlight seem gay, strong and purposeful. In certain forms and connections they are also described as bold (especially when used in clothing); but there is another series, so-called secondary colours, produced by mixing the spectrum colours together or with black or white: grey-blue, brown, pink and that sort of thing. These are quieter – in certain connections one can say they are more delicate. In certain periods the simple colours have been considered barbaric and the secondary ones finer. Conversely, secondary colours may be considered anaemic and boring by those who have a more aggressive, zestful attitude to life.

Sometimes it is thought especially choice and refined to use a series of shades of the same colour either in one's clothes (from hat to shoes) or in one's room (textiles and furniture). This is because this is so obviously contrived and costly.

TEXTURE

The surface of anything has texture. The qualities of texture are perceptible to the touch. Some people shiver when they touch a flower pot or a brick, and even the *sight* of these materials can cause a slight shivering sensation. A piece of wood well smoothed either with sandpaper or wind and weather feels good to handle – and to look at. Walls of rough granite make an interior appear more confining and enclosing than walls of smooth granite – because one does not want to get close to it.

A composition of textures can have the same effect as a composition of colours. If you make a cube of marble and polish two opposite sides leaving the others rough, the effect will be very much the same as that in our experiment with white and red. The shape will no longer be so unambiguous.

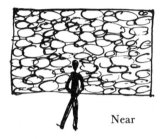

Near

In the same way, you can say that certain textures harmonize, just as certain colours do. A smooth silken material would be wrong on a table-top of sanded pine, but one of linen or wool would be right. Conversely, wool would be out of place on polished mahogany. If you are going to have contrasts they must be strong enough to strike you – like a table made of glass and chromium-plated steel standing on a shaggy carpet.

Far

What is quite smooth and shiny has something of the same effect as a really strong colour: it takes the attention away from the shape. The uttermost shininess is the mirror, which does not look like the flat surface it is, but just reflects something else. A shiny table-top will usually be a monstrosity because it destroys the impression of there being something definite and firm on which to place your cup or on which to work. On the other hand, the shiny and glossy can seem festive, like gay colours, especially in conjunction with roundness in shape. So can facetted things, where the facets give a varied reflection and thereby allow the shape to be properly in evidence.

Matt, clear surface

Our reaction to texture is rooted in practical experience and instinct. The surfaces of things emit signals that are caught by the eye, which transmits them to the spinal-

Shiny, unclear surface

Rococo, but here the shininess
helps to enhance the shape

cord and the nervous-system for deciphering. We can *see*
whether a material is soft or hard, brittle or tough, cold or
hot, and whether we like it or not. Against this background
we have become accustomed to there being several qualities of texture in one and the same thing: like the leaves of a
tree that are different on top and underneath; or a chest-
nut that protects its treasure by growing spikes to keep the
world at bay, while on the inside it is white, delicate and
smooth.

Modern technology has produced a number of highly
usable materials, especially plastics, that yet do not have
any direct appeal to the eye or to the senses. Natural
materials tell you something about themselves, even if you
do not actually see it, but these artificial products give you
a feeling of uncertainty and doubt; they seem foreign, cold
and dead.

Many people consider that subconsciously we will
suffer various deficiencies if our surroundings come to be
dominated by this kind of product. How far that will be
true in the long run remains to be seen – as so often
happens, perhaps any lack arising here can be compen-
sated by other means. At the present we can only say that
the tendencies that come under the heading *brutalism* and
which include great use of coarse concrete and natural
materials manufactured into something else must be
regarded as a reaction against the smoothness and glos-
siness of varnish, steel and plastic, all those featureless
materials that are produced by machines and chemical
plants.

The new moon – a sickle or a
sphere?

There is an old saying that in the dark all cats are grey. To this one might add that when it is *quite* dark, cats and everything else will disappear, for we won't be able to see them. Light is necessary if we are to apprehend form. This is such an obvious statement that it may seem hardly worth making. But when it is a question of arranging lighting so that something will stand out to the best advantage, there are so many problems that ought to be mentioned, that it is really best to start at the very beginning.

In order to comprehend a form it is necessary to have light, whether its source is the sun, a flame or an incandescent fitment. But if we are to have only one of these sources, then something more is needed, namely surroundings that can *reflect* this light from several angles so that it does not come from just one side. The moon is a good example of how badly one-sided lighting reproduces shape. A new moon looks like a sickle, the full moon like a disc – in neither case is it possible to see that what we are looking at is a sphere. This is because the moon hangs in empty space without neighbours to reflect sunlight, so that when the moon is new it is impossible to detect the parts not directly lit. And when the moon is full, the light on it is so evenly distributed that there are no shadows to indicate its spherical shape.

Incomplete lighting is only used in the theatre and cinema. It is then usually called dramatic, in the sense of exciting, just because it does not give a proper explanation of what is going on. This sort of lighting can be used to achieve the strangest effects. Look at the frontal view of the figure in the margin and the same figure lit from above so as to show what it really looks like, and then look at the same figure exposed to unreflected light from different sides. These are tricks – not lighting in the normal sense.

But it is not easy to achieve these exaggerated effects. In our surroundings there will almost always be something to reflect light back from several directions so that you can more or less grasp the whole. Obviously, it is not possible to make a general statement as to the most favourable

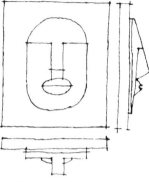

A figure

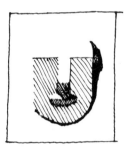

lit obliquely from above

obliquely from below

A figure lit directly from the side

and quite evenly

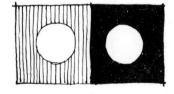

White is most dazzling on a
black background

lighting – it depends what it is you are lighting. One can only say that shadow is essential for full understanding, but that the contrast between the lightest and the darkest parts must not be too great and that the transition from one to the other should preferably be soft.

This is best achieved with daylight. Indoors, that means windows facing in more than one direction and walls that are relatively light in colour and thus reflect well. This is of course not meant to be taken as a rule for how rooms should be – there are so many other factors. Where the light is artificial, it is mainly a question of having a suitable number of lamps of the requisite strength suitably placed. And as it is particularly lamplight that we can control, we shall give most of our attention to that.

The most difficult thing about lighting a room and designing light fittings is the phenomenon known as *dazzle,* which is what happens when one looks directly at a source of light or a very bright surface. When dazzled, one cannot distinguish anything, for the eye receives a shock that deprives it of the ability to see for a shorter or longer time.

It is important to remember that dazzle is something extremely relative. The unclouded sun always dazzles and is impossible to look at directly; yet even the light of a pocket torch can dazzle a nocturnal intruder if it is shone in his face. A large window-opening can never be disturbing in this way, but the tiny window in a prison cell makes it impossible to distinguish details on the walls surrounding it. Even a white patch on a black background can dazzle or at least make things flicker before your eyes.

The decisive factors governing dazzle are these: the absolute strength of the light source, but mainly its relative strength, its relation to its immediate surroundings. Add to this its extent and more or less sharp delineation. By hanging transparent, light curtains round a dazzling window-opening, you will smooth the transition to the dark of the wall and the eye will find this pleasing.

Such curtains are thus not purely decorative, as many people seem to think. Gather them in the middle of the window leaving the sides bare, as is occasionally done, though heaven knows why – and their effect will be the exact reverse of that intended.

You can look into the flame of a candle perfectly well, but an electric bulb with forty, sixty or a hundred times as much light concentrated in a little spiral filament is quite dazzling. What has to be done, if one is to be able to look at this light, is to have it spread over a larger surface, so that the amount of light per surface unit is sufficiently reduced. The first step in this direction is to have the glass of which the bulb is made matt or milky white. Now the light seems to be coming not from the filament, but from the much larger glass surrounding it. But even this will dazzle, and that can only be stopped by surrounding the bulb with a light-distributing agent of considerably larger size, for example another ball of white glass, a globe, which then makes it appear is if *it* were the source of the light.

The light will spread from this globe in all directions and the lamp will be much more pleasant to look at, while the actual light in the room will be roughly the same as if the bulb were unshaded. Some of the light, of course, will be absorbed by the material of the globe, but it is none-theless an advantageous arrangement. The rays of light do not pass straight through the glass, but are refracted to some degree in various directions and this, plus the greater area of the globe, gives a softer shadow.

Such a light is not what you could call charming, especially if it is the only one in the room. Its even distri-bution makes it characterless. Some people think it is made more flattering if you colour the glass of the globe, but in fact all you do then is exclude part of the light and its colour.

Another way is to use, instead of the globe, a funnel of some opaque material that opens downwards. This com-pletely eliminates any possibility of dazzle, but on the other hand the light comes only as a cone and the shadows inside its area are sharp. This concentration of light can be increased by making the inside surface of the funnel glossy and the funnel itself a shape that allows the largest

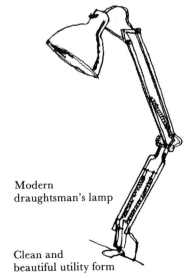

Modern draughtsman's lamp

Clean and beautiful utility form

In this case the direct lighting is better

Both lamps have opaque shades and are relatively inefficient

Shade tipped-up to give indirect lighting produces a dead light

possible proportion of the reflected rays to flood out through the opening. Fittings of this kind have a special use when a limited area has to be brilliantly lit and so are usually called reading- drawing- or work-lamps.

If you turn the funnel up the other way, so that it is facing a white ceiling, the source of light will remain invisible (as long as the funnel is above eye-level) and the whole room will be lit by the rays reflected from the ceiling. Using this *indirect* lighting the rays will go in innumerable directions and thus shadows will be obliterated and the whole effect will be soporific and dead. It is also a thoroughly uneconomic arrangement as it is only a fraction of the light produced that one has any benefit from. Nonetheless it can be used to advantage in conjunction with other more pronounced sources of light, when it merely provides a soft undertone of light in the room.

Current needs are most easily satisfied by surrounding the lamp with a shade of some translucent material (of these paper has the great advantage of being particularly refractive, though not very durable) shaped as a truncated cone that is open top and bottom. The shape is made of such a height and so placed that the bulb is not visible from anywhere one is likely to sit or be. Inside the remaining area the light can be allowed to pour freely upwards and downwards. In this way you get both a subdued general lighting, and to a certain extent also indirect lighting from the ceiling, while the strongest light is gathered under the lamp on the dining-table, desk, or whatever it is placed on. If it is a table with a light-coloured top or cloth, the effect of the lamp will be increased, and at the same time the difference between the more and less well lit parts will be enhanced and thus the room made more alive. It is wise always to hang and stand lamps as low as possible, as this produces the greatest effect where it is most needed.

Similar results can be produced more ingeniously and effectually by surrounding the bulb with a series of reflecting metal rings or small shades, made and arranged in such a way that the bulb remains hidden to the eye, yet part of the light gets out directly upwards and downwards, and part is reflected in the direction desired. This type of fitting perhaps makes the best lamp because there is no dazzle and they cannot wear out, as cloth or paper shades do, nor break as glass can.

Sunlight is made up of a series of colours, the ones we see when it is split into its components in a glass prism. It is this that enables us to apprehend corresponding colours in our surroundings. If the light from an ordinary electric bulb is passed through a prism, you will see that its spectrum does not contain so many colours – in other words there are certain colours we are prevented from seeing in such a light, which is thus *light of poorer quality*, but not so bad that it is not quite serviceable for everyday use.

There is, however another kind of lighting, called neon light, where the light does not come from a glowing filament, but from an incandescent gas. Its spectrum is very limited, containing just a few colours and the result is obvious: just look at the colour people's faces and hair go in the light of this modern wonder. Everything looks pallid and wan. This is bad quality light, but it has the advantage of being cheap, requiring less current, and the long tubes make it easier to distribute the light evenly where it is wanted. In offices and workshops and places where a lot of light is required and where areas are so large that you can use a combination of tubes with different gases and thus different spectra, the use of this type of light is defensible. But it is not for ordinary living rooms.

Good lighting has a lot to do with our comfort and efficiency; yet this is a sphere where thought and understanding are sadly lacking both in the positioning of lights and in the design of fittings. Most homes have far too few lights, whether this is due to misplaced economy or the misconception that this makes for a cosier atmosphere, whereas in reality it is merely depressing. A great many people seem to regard lamps more as decorative objects than things of use. Obviously they should be attractive, but in an appropriate, functional way.

On the other hand, it would be stupid to deny that light in itself is festive and can be used to enrich and decorate.

An efficient shade giving light on all sides

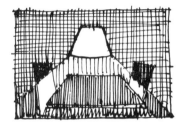

Lamp above a dark table top

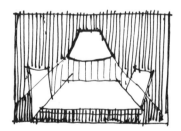

Lamp above a light table top giving greater efficiency-more light

55

Candles with their warm light and real flame have an undeniable attraction. However, lamps purely for visual pleasure are luxuries to be considered only after the *lighting* has been properly arranged.

In connection with what was said previously about the beneficial nature of grouping, it should be pointed out that lighting is one of the best ways of linking the parts of a living room.

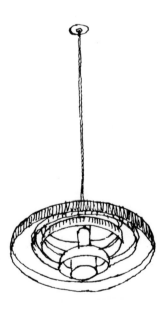

Modern metal shade – great efficiency, no dazzle

Chapter Seven HOW WE SEE THINGS AND
FACTORS THAT INFLUENCE US

Beauty, it is said, is in the eye of the beholder and that goes for other things as well. Psychologists are reputed to be able to discover a person's mental state by getting him to say what figures he sees in chance splodges of ink.

The qualities that lines, shapes, surfaces, colours and light have, and which we have already discussed, can on the whole be regarded as absolute, or at all events influenced by definite, ascertainable circumstances; that is to say that they are always valid – for Archimedes and for the girl serving in a boutique. It is different with the question of what we regard as ugly or good-looking which so far we have only discussed where we felt we were on safe ground.

In the case of the hats of those women in the bus, the observing eye was that of a person trained to grasp visual phenomena, in both their abstract content and their relation to various spheres of interest. Nonetheless it is not impossible that her assessment was wrong and that closer acquaintance with the underlying motives would have altered her opinion of what she saw.

It has often been pointed out that our opinion of things is marked by our knowledge of them. If we are asked to copy a few words written in our own language, we can do it straight off and without having to keep referring to what we are copying. But if the words are in a foreign language, to say nothing of a strange alphabet, we will feel highly uncertain of our ability to do so, unless we can take our time and have a method that presents hope of the result being accurate. We certainly shall not be able to do so at our normal speed of writing, simply because we have no idea which elements are the important characteristics of the various squiggles. Or, to put it differently: we do not really know what it is we are looking at. (We discussed something similar when dealing with our reactions to the appearance of tools.)

Now, handwriting is very special, but a good example of how there is the same relationship between opinion and knowledge in the world of objects is provided by streamlining. This is a product of exact knowledge and on this basis it also has its significance as pure form. But a hundred years ago such an aerodynamic form would not have told anyone anything. If it had cropped up in any connection it would not have aroused associations or emotions in anyone: people would have thought it meaningless, that is to say ugly.

When we first became conscious of it in connection with the technique of flying, a strange thing happened in that it was used in the design of things that were not made to fly, such as prams, meat-mincers, fountain pens and flower vases. Many people (including the author) thought this meaningless and irritating, and it was undeniably a confusion of ideas. But considering it further, now that it is no longer the fashion, it must be admitted that the phenomenon was not so pointless after all. A discovery had been made, some new thing had been learned that proved to be miraculously serviceable, and basically it was only reasonable that the symbol of such a discovery should be popularized and made use of.

To complete the picture let us have a look at an airport with its criss-cross of shorter and longer runways with narrower communicating strips between them. A number of lines in roughly this pattern will today arouse certain associations or seem to have a certain meaning for most people, while previously they would have been just a scribble.

These examples of changing ways of looking at things refer to conditions that are both fully comprehensible and immediately acceptable. But the circumstances attending our reactions can be considerably more complicated and make it difficult to discover to what extent the reaction is justified.

A man comes back from a trip abroad with a chair which he had thought unusually nice. It does not make any difference in this case whether it was an ingenious and expensive chair designed by a world-famous Italian or a

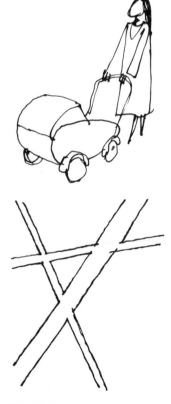

Streamlining as applied to the wing of an aeroplane and imitated in a pram!

Just lines? or an airport?

primitive peasant-made chair found in a joiner's shop somewhere in Greece and acquired for a few drachmae. The man's delight in his find is genuine and if he is even more proud of it when he finds that no one he knows has a chair like it, there is nothing wrong in that.

A few years later, the chair is discovered by a manufacturer and importer and then everybody has one like it and the man's delight in his possession is considerably diminished. But the chair surely looks just the same? That is a difficult question to which you can answer both yes and no.

It is not just a question of vanity. Our idea of what looks *especially* nice will always be linked with a desire for a certain degree of uniqueness. That is to say: our eye is extra receptive to impressions that are not ordinary, everyday ones, to things that are unusual. As soon as a thing can be seen here, there and more or less everywhere, it loses this attraction. And if one has to endure the sight of an object encountered everywhere, it must be something that is not in itself peculiar, because otherwise it will just appear obtrusive.

Our whole high standard of living is based on industrial mass production; in other words we are obliged to a large extent to surround ourselves with things of standardized design and appearance. Of course, these things should also be good-looking, but the very numbers of them in existence require that they be so in a very unobtrusive, anonymous way. Far from being a question of indifference, this requirement calls for great skill coupled with humility in the designer – something that it has taken a long time to realize.

Just as our ability to see is sharpened by rarity (where this does not seem frightening), it can be diminished by familiarity, whether it is of the mass-produced product, or something which people in all ages have been accustomed to have around them. This last is well illustrated when in your attic you come across an object which, after long being a part of daily life, had then been consigned to oblivion. Seeing it, you exclaim: Is *that* what it looks like? Many habit-bound husbands are irritated by their wives'

Good-looking chair

Not so good-looking now?

Even the person who likes the first spoon better might well prefer the second, if everyone else owned one like the other.

Arrangement of ornaments which a designer might well find distasteful

liking for changing the furniture around. Here they are silly. It is true enough that change is not always an improvement, in the objective sense, but it does help to maintain the pleasure one takes in one's things. When change delights, it is not just as a satisfaction of a form of restlessness.

It should be obvious that our opinion of the good and bad sides of things depends on circumstances and our attitude to life. This means that our opinions may change with environment – a principle which we find perfectly comprehensible when applied to the African jungle or ancient Egypt. We can take as much pleasure in an old home-made wooden spoon in the Museum of Folk Art as in the wonderful speciments of silver and glass in the Museum of Industrial Art. We know, or assume, that in all these cases the person who made the object was giving of his best and this we regard as decisive. We feel it right that these things *illustrate* their respective environments.

One of the most interesting aspects of this question of people's attitudes to the ugly and the lovely, is that of the extent to which we still can or should tolerate differences in the forms of its expression in various circumstances. It was this that made the observer in the bus doubt her right to say that hats of a certain category were ugly.

One of the hats we have been discussing was remarkably cheap and another remarkably expensive. We said then that the fact that they had been selected did not indicate either poverty or indifference on the one hand or affluence and vanity on the other.

To understand the motives that can have decided the choice of these hats, let us play safe and assume that both the women in question were in the same income group and that neither was particularly mean or extravagant, that both could be called cultured and that their hats were becoming, even though one was more modest and self-effacing than the other. How they looked otherwise does not concern us, nor are we illustrating them – the quality we are discussing cannot be conveyed in a drawing.

Newsprint is good enough for newspapers

We can best arrive at the heart of the matter, by starting with some general considerations: if people are to be able to accept the things that are made they must satisfactorily answer the need they are intended to satisfy, when viewed against the background of the practical possibilities. That means that any object, whatever it may be, demands the closest attention from both the producer and the designer; though obviously the thought given to it will vary according to whether we are dealing with buckets or wedding dresses. Practical requirements will dominate with the bucket, while with the wedding dress the practical aspect will be overshadowed by what one might call spiritual supplementary values. You can also say that these things will be approached with different feelings both by their makers and those who use them. So far, surely, everyone will be agreed?

Between these two extremes, however, there must be a mass of considerations whose emotional rating, and place in the total picture, will be difficult to establish and which, indeed, have changed through the centuries as circumstances and times have altered.

Parts of a trousseau

One might think that there always has been a direct connection between an object's function and the wish to give it a more or less ornamental appearance – so that in all ages what is downright utilitarian has always been associated with a correspondingly prosaic appearance, while supplementary values have been kept for the things that are more ceremonial and social. But this has not always been the case. An example of what is almost the opposite is the old smoothing board of Scandinavia which was once used to smooth and press clean linen. For all its utilitarian place in everyday life it was often decorated with a wealth of carving and given handles shaped like horses or lions. On the other hand, no one ever produced an ornamental version of the roller-mangle that succeeded the smoothing board.

A spoon for ladling porridge into one's mouth can also and rightly be called a thoroughly prosaic and material-istic tool. Even so people have expended a lot of imagina-tion and skill on making it much more than that. Made in silver such eating utensils have often been a family's proudest and most valuable possession. But, of course, you can say that they embody a certain symbolism linked with meals, the saying of grace, feasting and drinking of healths.

Furniture at its simplest can be just a chair, table, bed or cupboard, or it can be splendid and magnificent. But it can never be *just* one or the other. Furniture provides the clearest example of how obvious function is not all-decisive in design, and of how the need for supplementary values can be linked with the practical and efficient – or run parallel with it.

To get a clear picture of this important subject let us ask a bride to arrange all her trousseau in a row, not according to the monetary value of the various articles, but according to what she feels about them. The bucket will no doubt be at one end and her wedding dress at the other. Close to the bucket one might see a vacuum cleaner and a fridge, things she is delighted to have, yet not ones for which she has any personal feelings. Next perhaps will come a sofa, carefully chosen but more with regard to its

A smoothing board – more than just a tool

neutral, impersonal qualities. It is to be used as part of a greater, more meaningful whole. But after a certain point the things will give the young woman more real pleasure and delight, and she will look upon them as expressing her personality and her attitude to life. These could start with a pretty casserole, and so on up to her dress, next to which is perhaps some treasured piece of jewelry.

It is on these points that we should focus our attention. It will be obvious that the recipient's standard of living and attitude will influence both the place in the row that each object is given and the sort of thing that is on either side of it.

To return to the woman with the cheap hat: her hat was not a matter of indifference to her: she had an eye for style, but otherwise stuck to what in her personal opinion was *good enough.* One can assume that she required mental supplementary values in only a limited number of every-day things and that hats were, at best, on the borderline of this field. Perhaps she would much rather concentrate her interest and money on a trip to Ravenna to see the mosaics.

Her moderation corresponds to a definite tendency in modern architecture and house-furnishing. People are no longer as concerned that the individual pieces should be pretentious, but rather that they be regarded as tools, good enough to serve the purpose but not necessarily more. The supplementary values can come in the way they are assembled and in connection with quite other things.

You often see this doctrine put into practice in the homes of young designers and architects, where the furniture may consist of plain mattresses, rough stools and lampshades made of cartridge paper, that is to say of things that people with greater social ambitions consider beneath them because they equate the cheap with the degrading and so cannot appreciate its true appearance. Conventional considerations, especially in conjunction with what is regarded as social status symbols, are among the greatest obstacles in the way of an impartial appreci-ation of beauty.

A stove like a temple, made in Ulefos, Norway, about 1800

A radiator

A treasured object and something that is functional, but no more

Chair, showpiece of 1900

Chair, mass-produced in 1950. Good enough?

Which did the most work go into?

Now we come to the expensive hat.

Its high price was not due to it having been *created* by one of the famous milliners who can command enormous fees, but, in the first place, was due to the unusually high quality of the felt and the careful hand-sewing – a thing that the woman in question appreciated. On the whole she found continual pleasure in being surrounded by exquisite things, things that were the best that were to be had. To achieve this, she was prepared to demand less in other spheres – like trips to Ravenna and that sort of thing.

This woman could be called an aesthete, a somewhat outmoded term that applies to all who crave beauty, but in normal parlance is applied first and foremost to those who regard things as inferior unless they satisfy the highest requirements you can make in respect of quality. They regard porcelain as especially lovely when it is as thin and translucent as possible. If you put a piece of embroidery in their hands they will examine each stitch before pronouncing themselves satisfied. They do not recognize the term *good enough;* the only thing that counts is the *best.*

Handmade glass (tough, soft mass) Hand-beaten silver (tough and hard) Handmade pottery jug (soft)

Connection between shape and
material

People with this attitude of mind reveal a quite new
aspect of the nature of beauty, that is that beauty can
consist in being exceptional in the sense of being made
superbly and with impressive skill. Most people find this
exemplified in fine-detailed work like engraving on jewels
or miniature painting on snuff-boxes. It is more difficult
for the untrained to recognize it in a handbag, the leather
of which comes from a particular kind of buffalo and
which is sewn by a masterly hand – but the aesthete might.

To a certain extent you can equate quality and beauty,
and all yearning for refinement and perfection must be
accorded sympathy. It is an attitude, however, that can
lead one astray – things are not necessarily good-looking
because they have been made with great expenditure of
effort. The converse can also be true: a typical caricature
of this is the model of Cologne cathedral someone built of
234,000 matchsticks as a hobby.

The enemy of quality is kitsch. Modern technology in
this respect has sorely tried the aesthete and presented
him with perplexing problems of judgment. Is a genuine
pearl really so much more beautiful than an artificial one?

Is a handbag of real leather so greatly to be preferred to one of plastic, if the latter is just as durable and as well made?

In many cases you can say that natural materials, genuine ones, stand up to wear more worthily, that use to a certain extent enobles them – as a Stradivarius can only retain its wonderful qualities when it is regularly played. But that is not always the case. One must however admit that things that do not perform what they promise, that break despite the fact that they looked solid, are inferior. They make us feel cheated and rightly so. Things that pretend to be what they are not must be placed in this category, even when the quality of them, from the technical point of view, is the same. We want to know what it is that we are seeing. Things that make us feel uncertain in this respect, are ugly.

The women with the cheap hat and the expensive hat can be said to represent two opposite points of view, at all events as long as we are concerned with everyday things, though both display thought and adopt a conscious attitude. Their attitudes show that our views of the ugly and the good-looking can also be based on a different kind of *morality,* on our idea of what is to be regarded as worthwhile in life and how one is to express one's attitude to it.

Petit point
Laborious handwork can give
birth to special, aesthetic
qualities, but not always!

Chapter Nine THE CONVENTIONAL AND THE CONCEPT CALLED STYLE

Man, notoriously, has an urge to emit articulate sounds, which are also known as speech. Usually the purpose is to communicate something, to express feelings or ideas. And even when there is no actual meaning in what is said, which does happen, we still talk simply in order to show that we exist.

When we surround ourselves with things of a certain character, we do so, among other reasons, as a supplement to speech, to assert ourselves in this way too, preferably also to give expression to certain opinions on this, that or the other matter. Although there may be a great deal that we think lovely, for our own use we will make a definite selection, that is of the things we think we especially need both in the practical and intellectual sense. The moment these things have become *ours*, they acquire a fresh content. We not only take them to our hearts, we also hold them out to the world as expressions of ourselves, confirmation of our personalities.

The director at his desk

The woman with the loud red hat perhaps wanted thereby to tell the world (and at the same time to convince herself) that she was a daring, devil-may-care person. Here her hat is a better means of expression than speech, because she can hardly go round *saying* such a thing about herself, especially not to strangers in a bus.

In this case the connection between the qualities of the hat and its wearer is easy to see. The perspicacious observer was also able to see a connection between the attitude-to-life and the hat of the two where the question of quality was the most marked. But this takes us only part of the way – choice of *shape* must surely be able to tell us something too.

If, for example, it had transpired that the woman with the conical hat was a mathematician you could have said that that was an obvious expression of her personal interests, and the whole thing would have been simple and

Status symbol

We like to be like

and fear what is strange

easily comprehensible. But as a rule it is not as simple as that. One might take such a demonstration as an example of professionalism carried to idiocy (maybe a polyhedron would make a more comfortable covering). Mathematicians ought to realize that there are other values in life than those connected with their science.

Man has a complex nature and so is often divided against himself. There are thousands of examples of this, but here is just one concerned with the decisive ability to organize society, submit to division of labour and responsibility. This has been an important factor in making it possible for us to achieve the prosperity we have and all that goes with it. If everyone had to make do on his own, we would still be living in caves.

For many of us, however, this division of labour means that we have to suppress an urge for freer development. In addition it must inevitably result in some people being better off than others – no order will ever be entirely right or just, however eager the favoured are to convince others that this is the case. Nor are the unfortunate able to protest and struggle against the superior force of the others *all the time;* one is better off thinking that everything in the garden is lovely rather than being tormented by dissatisfaction. The result is that all parties, at any rate at certain times, display great eagerness to discover stabilizing elements or to establish a sense of unanimity.

Even though we have a wild beast inside us that every now and again tries to escape from the cage of concord and solidarity, the social instincts are far and away the strongest. Most people feel safest and most at ease, when they have the impression that everyone in the main thinks, feels and behaves as they are accustomed to do – the contrary case is disturbing. One of the things people do to support this feeling of security is to establish a common style. This means that from a multiplicity of forms and shapes they select a group of related ones – those they feel best illustrate the desired common attitude – and use them as long as this is possible.

To show how distinct and different these style-patterns can be, let me briefly describe examples from two periods

Cabinet

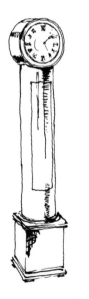

Clock made of two cylinders and a cube

of history, the one called *baroque* which assumed its especial characteristic forms towards the end of the seventeenth century, and *neo-classical* which characterizes the beginning of the nineteenth century.

Baroque was the era of absolutism and the stress was laid on *power*. People also had a vast appetite for life and were very self-confident. This resulted in houses being built at the end of long, straight streets or avenues in order to make them look really impressive. Decorations were lavish, with swelling, enfolding forms; chairs had tall high backs that made the person seated on them look more impressive, and people wore wigs, stiff coats and high-heeled shoes; everything looked sumptuous and grand.

In the neoclassical period (the time of the First Empire) it was the bourgeois middle-class that set the style. They were not so wealthy, more careful about the use they made of their money, strictly moral, correct and punctilious, with academic education being what gave status. This resulted in a worship of severe line and pure, geometric forms. The pompous was now considered vulgar. Things, they thought, should be unostentatious, but all the more obviously permeated with intellect. Chairs became slender, no unnecessary material being used, and they were deliberately made uncomfortable to sit on so as to prevent anyone adopting a sloppy undignified posture. Women's dresses became simple shifts and men dressed in black.

Both these periods, however, have this in common, that they clearly betray man's urge to *master* the situation, to fashion his surroundings on the basis of ideals he has *thought* out, of abstract notions of order and method. In order to show that they would not submit to the fortuitous, they established and subordinated themselves to the tyranny of form and the behaviour patterns that went with it.

Both, of course, apply in the first place to the élite, the ruling classes. The houses and furniture of the petite bourgeoisie, of the country people and fishermen, were different and more stable in character. The currents of fashion could be noticed there only as a surface ripple, if

Room at Maihaugen, Norway

Cupboard with Renaissance
motifs, Normandy.
In the unchanging peasant
milieu, styles acquire a different
resonance.

at all. Nevertheless, here too there was a definite order of things, though in contrast to the prevailing attitude this was far more a case of *conforming*. Such people cut their coats according to their cloth, as one says, and not heedlessly. Practical requirements and the way in which the family's life was organized were elevated to an articulate plane, thoughtfully adjusted with everyone participating in accordance with principles that were more functional than formal.

These reflect not only two different milieux, but also two sides of man's complex nature, though strictly speaking one cannot say that one is more or less human than the other: on the one hand is the urge to govern and play a part that is deliberately assumed, while on the other hand is man's ability more or less directly to make the best of the prevailing situation. Both attitudes have their negative sides: in the directions respectively of the highfalutin' and the undisciplined – it is not easy being human.

The Middle Ages was an era characterized by the conforming way of life, and thus ordinary architecture and furnishings of this period do not have a characteristic style in the same demonstrative way as do baroque and neoclassical. The fact that nevertheless there was a distinct kinship between everything that was made then, was much more because they used the same common traditions and methods of craftsmanship. The cohesion of the whole picture was thus more organic than formal, while the picture itself was more homogeneous than it was in subsequent periods, that is to say: lacking any distinction in principle between the form language of the upper classes and that of the people.

The present day seems to have adopted mainly a similar attitude of acceptance towards the problems: that is to say we try to solve each individual task by responding to its distinctive quality, with the main emphasis on the practical side. This is a direct result of our democratic social system and the fact that the social developments and the violent increases in population have created a vast number of new needs. If these are to be satisfied to any degree, we have to set about things rationally, exploiting

Architect's home, 1940. Here there is no *style* in the narrow sense of the word.

Some shapes endure. Chairs like this could be found in any European country in the last 4–500 years.

our resources by the most economical and effective means. On the assumption that the individual should be able to develop as freely as possible, we at the same time seek to avoid means that standardize and pave the way for definite behaviour-patterns.

Seen against this background the concept of *style* is not so desirable as one had imagined, for the simple reason that it is an expression of comprehensive standardization. Though style may have acted as a support for most people, it must through the ages also have acted as a compulsion. Under the Empire, for example, there must have been many people whose temperament was strongly opposed to the official ideals and accompanying strict style-pattern of the day, and whose development was thereby inhibited.

It would be reckless, and indeed scarcely possible, to try and free each other of style. Most of us, indeed, continually long for a pattern of living, a support to lean on, a co-ordinating element. It is not easy to live without supports of this kind, there are too many decisions to be taken on one's own, ranging from whether to be confirmed to how to furnish your living room.

It is for this reason that many designers still try to make their houses resemble those designed by the few trend-setters in the profession. The same applied to most of the women in the bus; even if their own deliberations were lengthy and painful, the deciding word was not theirs.

There are many reasons why there is today such confusion in people's ideas of the ugly and the beautiful, even while most people are occupied with such ideas more perhaps than ever before.

In the first place, it is a reflection of the considerable confusion that prevails in almost all other spheres. We are in the middle of a process of development and the upheaval is such that no one can properly envisage how the world will look in a few years time. But there are plenty of indications that we will be compelled to change our opinions of many things, including ugliness and beauty.

The consequences of modern production-processes are very much in evidence here. Indeed, they have already been creating chaos for a good hundred years and have led to endless artistic and philosophical speculation over how they are to be met – with adequate precautions say some, with delighted applause say others. Our social upheaval has also upset transmitted concepts. This we have already mentioned, but let us now go into it a little farther.

To correct one's ideas can be a difficult process for the individual, though it is regarded as almost a matter of course in the relationships between the generations. The upheavals in the cultural situation of the sixteenth century, which we call the Renaissance, gave rise to a strong tendency to get away from mediaeval architecture, which was now considered barbaric. Gothic was a term of opprobrium derived from the Goths who with the Vandals had wrought such destruction in the fourth and fifth centuries. Other periods have been given contemptuous names. The word baroque originally meant irregular and improbable and rococo, fanciful. In the 1930s practically everything that belonged to the past was regarded with scepticism by radical designers, to whom it was at the best uninteresting.

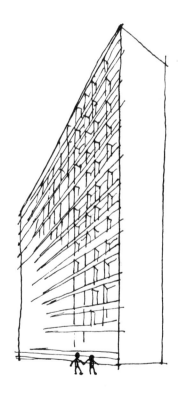

Today's situation is not without its problems

75

When things recede further into the past, this lack of tolerance appears petty, if not stupid – *we* can of course see the beauty in the products of the Middle Ages and the Renaissance. And even if we personally feel more attracted by one or other of those periods, we must regard their performance as equal or, more correctly, as not comparable.

In times of transition, however, it is a sheer necessity to turn one's back on the accomplishments of previous generations, representing as they do opinions and attitudes one is attempting to eradicate.

The experience of our own century has shown that much of what is asserted in such connections can prove to be pure nonsense when looked at more closely. But when people are fighting, they are not so particular about the means they use. Likewise, time often shows that what has been said in defence of something new will not hold water – one forces oneself to esteem highly the still inarticulate expressions of new ways of thinking. Doubt has to be stifled even if that involves using irresponsible means.

It is only when the fight has been won in principle that one can look more calmly and carefully both at one's own accomplishments and those of the previous period. Many of those who took part in the struggle for functionalism have since shaken their heads sorrowfully and regard it as retrogression when they see the frills of the 1880s and the convolutions of Art Nouveau coming back into fashion. But there is no real need for anxiety – these are just surface phenomena, things one can toy with just because they no longer constitute a danger or are things one really believes in. One can also regard these tendencies as readjustment of the strongly dogmatic programme of functionalism.

The changing ideas of what is ugly and what lovely, with which we are dealing now, thus have nothing to do with absolute values of beauty – but are based on the *opinions* the things represent. Of course, it is not inconceivable that in certain periods people's sense of form is on a lower level than at others. Individuals are differently equipped in this respect, so why not whole societies? One can also see how from country to country art has found

Obviously one must often dissociate oneself from the recent past.

76

more or less fertile ground in different periods.

This, however, answers only one aspect of the question. It is very largely possible to make a quantitative assessment of beauty as long as you are dealing with products of the same character made with much the same end in view. Whether a thing is more or less good-looking can only be judged by comparing it with something that is on the whole homogeneous.

You have to tread delicately when setting up to judge whole periods. Anyone is perfectly free to hold the opinion that the people who created the baroque style were delightful and those of the First Empire boring and to find a corresponding joy in the style of the one and to loathe that of the others. But to proceed from there and assert that the neoclassical is worse than the baroque is too big a step altogether. To do so would just be to betray a quite unjustifiable confidence in one's own judgment and to proclaim one's own state a sort of norm. But no one knows what the normal person or his art-development is like. And a good thing too.

You get the most out of the products of the past by regarding them all as expressions of the different sides of man's complex nature; that is, as different sides of one's own being, both those one admits and those one tries to hide out of regard for the atmosphere of the day, or which are suppressed by a certain temperament. We all go about with a baroque prince inside us, tiny though he may be, and a certain religious sense is aroused in even the godless man when he enters a Gothic cathedral. But since every historical period, including the present, has distinguished itself by a certain one-sidedness – the reasons for which we have already discussed – it is only the collective picture of human development that can be considered in any way adequate.

If you adopt this attitude you will find that *everything* from the past, whether building or furniture that is still being used, or things that have landed in museums, do seem to be good-looking – more or less, of course, but at all events they are never ugly. This makes one wonder whether people used to have a much sounder sense for good

Art Nouveau, long despised but now in fashion again

Even the godless . . .

design than of people today who, the experts will tell you, are regrettably deficient in this respect. That does not sound probable, but . . .

This idea finds a certain justification in the fact that when craftsmen made things individually there was a different and far more intimate contact between producer and buyer than there is when things are made by machines. People must have been much better able to judge the technical quality of a thing in those days simply because there were fewer possibilities. Also, slower development provided greater stability and greater familiarity with the language of form.

The decisive thing about *our* reactions to the products of the past, however, is that we judge them from the viewpoint not of their age, but of ours. The fact that we do not think these old things ugly is because they do not impinge on contemporary situations and there is no need to protest against the opinions they represent, since they do not threaten our own attitude – provided the distance in time is great enough. Nor do we know all the circumstances that make up the background of these things, do not know how far one could have asked for a better (better-looking) job to have been made of it.

That is why one can even go into the poorest rooms in a Folk Museum without feeling anger or pity for the conditions of which they tell. On the contrary, we feel that this poverty has a certain refinement about it, a quality which is lacking in many manifestations of contemporary affluence. Such a romantic attitude finds a certain justification in the fact that even the most humble of these old rooms in a way bears the stamp of an independent culture of its own, tells of efforts to make the best of the prevailing situation. It may be poor, but it is not shoddy.

The people of those days saw things differently. The poor thought they were poorly off, and for the élite likewise ugly was synonomous with cheap and primitive. What was homely and of the people was regarded with contempt or, at the best, as picturesque, which was the attitude at the end of the eighteenth century before national romanticism tipped the scales the other way. But by

In the craftsman's workshop . . .

. . . and in a shop

Romantic rationalism discovers
rural art

The whatnot as a support for
junk: the syndrome of the
industrial era

then the situation was becoming entirely different, both
where society and the technology of production were
concerned.

Suddenly there were machines producing for next to
nothing things which it would have taken a craftsman
weeks or months to make. Not *quite* the same, not quite as
good as those made by hand, but not all that much worse.
On the other hand, some machines could makes things
that no artisan could ever have made. This, plus the other
reason already mentioned, resulted in people filling their
homes with all sorts of useless junk to make it look as if they
were well off. Although somewhat unbalanced, this was a
completely understandable exploitation of the situation.

What was worse in the eyes of the intellectual was that the peasant discarded the wooden ladle he had himself made, and perhaps even carved, in favour of a cheap mass-produced metal one. If you say that this denotes a decline in people's sense of quality you may be right, but if you condemn the peasant's action as a betrayal of his cultural duties you will be on anything but safe ground. For, obviously, the new ladle must in his eyes have been more admirable, an exceptional product lovelier than his own and also considerably more useful. But clearly such things must cause confusion in the scales of values we have been discussing.

Anyone of sensibility will shudder at the sight of a three-and-ninepenny plastic vase pretending to be rococo porcelain; but it is worth pointing out that the shudder, like most of our other reactions to beauty and ugliness, is based on *knowledge,* in this case of what rococo really is. One is, as it happens, justified in supporting the condemnation of this plastic vase as trash. In this case it is also easy to damn its shape and decoration as *bad,* because it can be compared to a very much finer model.

THE CULTURE GAP

Today's greatest problem in this battle between the ugly and the lovely thus lies on the social plane and is linked with what is called the culture gap.

There have always been gaps between the social strata and the ideas held by those in them, but previously no one bothered about it much. The gap was well nigh insuperable and those on the popular side were largely compelled to meet their needs from their own resources. They had – or were – their own painters, carpenters, potters, blacksmiths and builders. Those on the other side of the gap for long ages considered that they had done their cultural duty by the common man, if they had taught him to spell his way through the Catechism.

The advent of popular democracy, new methods of production, newspapers, wireless and television has changed all that. Everyone has his material and intellectual needs satisfied by these same factories, rotary presses

The fateful hour of rural culture

and broadcasting stations, so that the conditions in which an actual folk culture could exist have virtually disappeared. Strictly speaking this is not to be regretted, since that possibility was based on social and sometimes geographic isolation and material poverty.

In this situation the authorities (that is to say, the faceless representatives the common man theoretically has elected) feel a wide responsibility for the general level of culture which is based on education and various institutions for the promotion of intellectual interests. Idealists within the different professional groups, among them designers, endeavour to develop in their fellow men understanding of the values involved in what they are doing. Everyone ought to be elevated to the same level, which is a lovely idea.

The only problem is that these representatives of culture, being better educated, are members of a distinct milieu, characterized by distinct needs that are different from those that have to be met in other milieux. This results in a clash of interests that becomes particularly obvious just where one is trying to please everyone.

The working man in front of his TV is annoyed and irritated by an absurd play by an avant-garde playwright which has nothing to say to him, not impinging on *his* attitude to life. As he is helping to pay for the stupid nonsense he conceives a mistrust of everything that passes under the name of *culture*. The next programme is one of light entertainment and the intellectual who has been sitting in front of *his* set enjoying the play, is now nauseated by what he considers to be arrant rubbish. His nausea will probably be justified, because this is not an expression of a *different kind* of cultural situation, but of something that is *worse*, more inane than it need be. Instead of being two forms of expression, the total picture seems rather to offer a right side and a wrong.

The same thing applies to the world of objects, where the common man's needs are superficially met by the products of industry which are merely pretentious or rubbishy, cheap versions of the possessions of the élite – by which I mean on the whole an intellectual élite, since the

The box: syndrome of the twentieth century

possession of money is less than ever decisive for cultural status.

This impasse has lasted for centuries and there would seem to be only two ways out of it. The one way would be for all practising the arts and crafts to be better educated where their fellow men and their various needs are concerned. They would then also be able to meet those needs without at the same time thinking that they were compromising with their consciences.

The other way is for the individual to try to be more aware of his real needs and to find ways of directly influencing the apparatus of production. Here, the relatively new consumer organizations look as though they should be able to play an effective part. Their pronouncements, of course, can scarcely extend to questions of ugliness and beauty, but there is no need to regret that. The aesthetic will arrange itself, or so one must think, as soon as there are *any* grounds for making a judgment.

THE OLD

One particular characteristic of the present day is our respect, even preference for old things, for so-called antiques. There are two sides to this question: it can be interpreted as a regrettable lack of confidence in the abilities of one's contemporaries, or as a pleasing desire to include the past in our image of the world. It is healthy to be reminded that plenty of people have lived before us and that *our* way of life is not the only one.

It is, however, one thing to respect and honour, and quite another to copy. With regard to the latter, people hold strong views as to what is permissible and what not. Even when a copy is good, it must never try to fool you into thinking it is the real thing. To be taken in is ugly, and an unsuccessful attempt to take people in is just ridiculous. As a rule these attempts will not succeed, if only because the level of craftsmanship is not as high today as it used to be, but also because the work cannot possibly be approached in the same spirit. This becomes painfully obvious, especially in the attempts that are made to revive old peasant culture.

The heirloom

Someone may say that rococo furniture is more to his taste than modern furniture and so he prefers to surround himself with the former, either genuine pieces or reproduction. That is his private concern. But he must realize that his attitude will not seem convincing unless it also finds expression elsewhere, in his attitude to modern society and its benefits. And he must not feel hurt if a designer refuses to help him. It can only be depressing to be asked to make something that of its very nature cannot be better than what has already been made.

It is reasonable to be proud of old family possessions. Buying an antique can be an expression of natural pleasure, if it is done out of interest in the diversity of men and as a supplement to the contemporary one-sided interpretation of the situation. And someone who has five Louis xvi chairs and wants a sixth to complete a set to go round his dining table must surely be allowed to satisfy his sense of order, if he can find a skilled furniture maker to make one for him. What one must be on one's guard against, however, is the reluctance to engage in any effort to create a contemporary cultural pattern.

Old things should be used for
their intended purpose

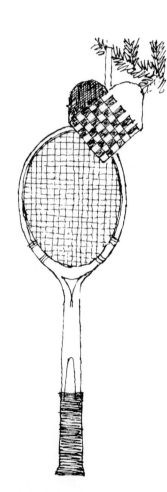

It is doubtful if anyone will ever be able to say precisely what it is that makes a piece of music, a book or a film good or bad. Again and again people have laid down rules for others to follow and for a time they may have been followed, then suddenly someone comes along and upsets them all. It then transpires that the rules were really a hindrance and that by breaking them something new and splendid has been achieved, something that in a rousing way reflects the new situations and gives people what they need *now*.

The something must necessarily apply to everything connected with forming our surroundings, whether great or small, and the accompanying opinions as to what is ugly and what good-looking.

But, of course, it has been possible to discover *some* irrefutable grounds and these I shall now enumerate; but first let us give a comprehensive survey of the qualities that can be attributed to things and the effects they have.

It has been established that things individually and in combination, can represent the concept *order*. And, as order and method together provide the basis for all culture, our reactions here are direct and strong. It has further been established that one can distinguish between practical-technical order and abstract order, which can again be divided into formal and organic.

In assessing things we next deal with their *quality*, that is to say whether they are skilfully made of suitable, durable materials. This objective must nevertheless be relative, depending on our ideas of what one can reasonably demand and on the role the object in question is going to have to play. In the case of Christmas decorations the requirements as to quality will be pretty modest, while the keen tennis player will be really demanding where his rackets are concerned. For him only the best will be good

Requirements as to quality
differ

enough, and in this case quality can have something of a specific aesthetic value.

Considerations of serviceability will be of roughly equal importance. Here too the question will be *how* serviceable the object is to be in the practical sense, whether its function is simple or complex and to what extent it is wanted to bring to light another idea-content at the same time.

Lastly, this idea-content can be conceived as the essential – the thing has then become the intermediary of sentiments or opinions that are more or less clear. A jug, shaped like a human head with a laughing face, is obviously meant to have a jovial effect. The potter has wanted to pass on his own gay mood to the jug's future owner via the jug. This is easily intelligible, so much so that the means can seem obtrusive and banal, in the long run intolerable, unless they are combined with very special, intellectual qualities.

Utensil with human associations

What we are most concerned with here, of course, are the means of expression in the abstract plane, those that make their point through form and line without directly representing or imitating something. It should be obvious now that they provide a large range to play on: things can seem static, radiate peace and quiet harmony, or they can express movement, appear dynamic and exciting to the point of being aggressive. Things can be made to appear heavy, hard and grave, or soft, light, friendly and glad. They can possess all sorts of physical attitudes from the powerful and resilient on the one hand to the graceful and pleasingly relaxed on the other. For that matter they can also be slack and inert, which no one, I imagine, will find attractive.

Sometimes it can be difficult to make clear distinctions between the qualities that arise directly out of form and those that acquire meaning by reminding the beholder of something. Take jugs again, this time one that does not represent a fat man, yet reminds you of just that, whether you regard the fact as attractive, comical or repulsive. Reminders of this kind can be still regarded as perpetually valid and beyond discussion because they refer to Nature.

Silver coffee pot of the 1880s
The intention was to remind the
Norwegians that they are
descended from Vikings and to
endow them with
correspondingly fearless qualities

On the other hand, if you say that a house is ugly because it reminds you of a cigar-box, that is not a very valid argument, in that it assumes that cigar-boxes must arouse general feelings of dislike, which they do not. The real meaning of the comparison must be that houses and cigar-boxes ought to have individual characters to avoid any risk of confusing them, but then, the risk of this is so slight as to be non-existent. If you want to persist in a negative attitude to the house, you must try to find a more relevant grievance. And if you cannot, it could mean that your condemnation had been overhasty.

It may be more difficult to overlook reminders of a personal or chance nature. One person may hate the sight of a particular sewing-table because it is the same as one his Aunt Emma has and he can't stand Aunt Emma! No amount of reading about what is ugly and what not will change his opinion on this point; that would probably call for a psychiatrist, if there were any need. There's more call, in fact, to rid oneself of *pleasant* memories – for example heavenly holidays in grandmother's old house, because these might cause you to believe that you still feel best in similar surroundings, while in reality they no longer suit your changed situation.

There is another connection into which problematical social aspects enter. People who are not too well off often like to surround themselves with the things which the better off have round them, even though shortage of money and room may make this a burden both for their purse and their daily activities. Conversely, it might be said that such tendencies signify a natural ambition, and that the aim of architecture and design – including the design and furnishing of living rooms – is to idealize the situation. Thus, the individual would be well advised to weigh up his desires and needs as well as he can, putting everyday life and any class consciousness in one side of the scales and his ambitions in the other. He can then decide whether, say, it is worth his while to drive about in anything so ridiculous and sensible and unpretentious as the cheapest Citroën, a vehicle which looks like a bedstead on wheels.

Motorcar for the rich – in spirit

It is to be hoped that this has shown how much actual objects can have to tell, how much they can symbolize or express. Obviously they can never be made to express anything as complex as, say, Darwin's theory of evolution, but on the other hand what they say is much more direct. It can substantiate important sides of morality and attitudes to life, temperamental and emotional life, as well as acting as a manifestation of a standard of living and of acquired or inherited insight and accomplishment. It can also contain what cannot be expressed in ordinary words and which can be a source of profound joy.

On the basis of all that we have been saying, it should now be possible to list the criteria for what is good-looking. This is probably best done by first eliminating what does not look good, what we call ugly. Here, as we have seen, we have to do with two categories of ugliness, that is: what is ugly in the absolute sense and what is relatively ugly, what seems ugly because it does not fit in with the other conditions.

Ugly in the absolute sense is
everything that occasions physical feelings of
displeasure
and
all that is trashy and shoddy, that tries to look as if
it were better than it really is,
and
all that seems discordant, like a gold
ring in a pig's nose,
and
all mess and litter, all that is worn out or broken,
everything that tells of stupidity or lack of
consideration, everything that is evidently useless
for its purpose.
Or to put it briefly,
everything that in respect of intellectual and technical
quality has been made with less care and thought than
the nature of the task and available skills and
resources would have indicated.

One example of absolute ugliness would be the working

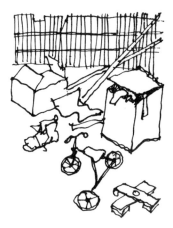

Indisputably ugly

These houses built in the 1880s
for the new industrial working
class have no redeeming features.
They are and will remain
inferior, that is to say, ugly.

class districts of industrial towns that were built in the last
century. They are ugly because they represent ugly
ambitions, as well as routine indifference in architectural
thought, because they tell of a task that was never perform-
ed and also because the are notoriously unhealthy.

When today's far healthier dormitory towns seem ugly
as well, it is because we know that our resources would
have allowed us to produce something better, if only they
had been employed with sufficient insight and thought.

The absolutely ugly from the remoter past is less obvious, partly because much has disappeared for natural
reasons, being inferior, and partly because we cannot
judge the relevant situations, since we are unfamiliar with
the ideas behind it all and the possibilities that existed
then.

Ugly in the relative sense is
everything that represents an opinion, an attitude to
life, from which for certain reasons we desire to
dissociate ourselves.

As a rule everything from the preceding age will be considered ugly just for that reason, whether we are direct opponents of the spirit of the age it represents or because the age itself is considered an outdated stage in the process of development in which we ourselves are now more advanced. Of course, where most people are concerned, this dissociation will not be deliberate – because we will happily think that our own state provides a valid yardstick and find the things of the immediate past comical.

Dislike of what represents an opinion different from our own is usually more violent where quite new forms of expression are concerned. The person who has adjusted himself entirely to prevailing conditions finds these forms disturbing, simply because they are strange and incomprehensible, and because they represent a threat. That is why many of today's parents are disgusted by their own long-haired sons and why it is no use telling them that all men wore their hair long a couple of hundred years ago. Parents react in this way because their sons' hair is a challenge and a vote of no confidence in the world the young are being presented with.

Now we come to the good-looking.

Many of the chair designs of the 1930s provoked bitter dislike, because they were based on new ideas.

Good-looking in the absolute sense is
everything which has been made with the care, both intellectual and technical, appropriate to the nature of the task and its place in the whole.
Being good-looking presupposes order whether of technical, practical, formal or organic nature, individually or in combination.
Degree of beauty can only be registered by comparing performances accomplished under similar conditions and with similar aims.
The exceptional can be especially beautiful, but is not necessarily so.

Good-looking in the relative sense is
everything that helps to confirm our general ideas of what is right and proper. Even more attractive are the things that seem to foretell improvements to come.

Famous Adam interior (1762).
The experts are usually
agreed as to what is best in the
different historical periods.

Those with narrow horizons will find pleasure in the things
that can be fitted into that narrowness. Similarly, the
foresighted who are bent on the implementation of a
certain programme have to reject everything that does
not fit in with that programme. When times are calm and
harmonious, however, they will be able to allow themselves wider pleasures.

Man's self-respect and well-being depends on everything that is made being good-looking. Some people may
consider this an exaggeration, but instead of *good-looking*
say *well-made* or *fit for human beings* and it will at once appear acceptable. The good looks or beauty applicable to
the bucket or the mutual relation of the articles on a desk
or in the parcels office of a railway station will not provide
one with a great experience. Good looks will only be
apparent in the fact that everything is in order, arranged,
properly done.

Some things should be beautiful in the sense that to all intents and purposes you do not notice them, that they are as much taken for granted as trees and grass. They should not seem eager to speak or make themselves heard out of season. This so-called anonymous beauty is still to be found in the products of the ordinary workmen of backward countries. Yet the remarkable thing is that the professional industrial designer has the greatest difficulty in producing anything that is beautiful in this natural, unforced way; this is partly because he does not have the foundations of tradition for his work and partly because artistic education has until recently been aimed at fostering what is called personality.

The nature of beauty is infinite in its variety. The ideals of beauty of the Middle Ages and the Renaissance differed widely. When the first examples of functionalism were built people thought that nothing so ugly had ever been done before. Yet even though this may make it seem pretty well impossible to discover what are the distinguishing marks of the nature of beauty, there is one thing that is definite.

The experts have no difficulty in pointing out what is *best* from the various periods and here opinions have differed only very slightly from one generation to another. It may seem that everything is relative, but certain products will always be considered more valid than others. When all has been said, there does exist a common base for evaluation of beauty.

A lover of the baroque might not see beauty in a building like this.

During the last fifty years, largely as the result of the pioneering work of Ruskin and William Morris, persistent attempts have been made to influence the general public's ideas of what is ugly and what good-looking. To begin with the efforts were those of professionals, individually or through their associations, latterly the State has also taken a hand and today schools are also playing a part.

This zeal is new in our history. It is owing to the confusion whose causes we have already discussed. The aim would seem to be to develop people's ability to experience; to react to things impartially and spontaneously; and also to think independently and achieve a clearer idea of their own needs.

BAD

GOOD

Unfortunately, these efforts all too frequently have the contrary effect – in reality they often seem to aim more at getting everybody to think the same about everything, in this sphere as in so many others.

The blame for this discouraging situation is usually laid at the door of the mass-producers. But must not the idealists also accept some censure? The idealist by definition is not acting to further his own interests, while the job of the mass-producer here on earth is to make money. But another characteristic of the idealist is that he often moves in a world of unreality without acquainting himself with actual conditions; for which reason he can often let himself be content with superficial solutions.

It is obvious that nothing will have been gained by getting everyone to surround themselves with the right things – in the purely aesthetic sense – unless those who possess them are on intimate terms with them and really do consider them lovely. If this is not the case, you have only made bad worse by appealing to people's vanity and an unthinking desire to be in the fashion.

The propaganda of the 1930s to promote good design was inevitably one-sided.

Manufacturers stick to actual conditions and make things people want. The only fault to be found with this obliging behaviour is that they perhaps are over-eager – scarcely do people think that they have everything they need, before they are being tempted by hitherto unknown delights. Magazine advertisements tell wives that they can now buy as a Christmas present, for the man who has everything, a crutch such as those used by the disabled, except that it carries whisky flasks and tobacco tins. Bad taste is a mild expression for this sort of thing, but it is a good example of how our attitude to things should be determined by ethical as by aesthetic considerations.

In certain spheres it is possible to foretell accurately how things will develop. Submarines and space-rockets figured with surprising accuracy in science fiction long before they became reality. But to prophesy what people will think ugly or beautiful in ten years time is impossible. Forms that mean nothing at the present time may by then have shown that they contain something essential connected with a new way of thinking.

The only thing we can imagine is our *relationship* to things, that is to say our conception of their importance either practical or decorative.

One may be of the opinion that increasing affluence will knock the feet from under the puritanical programme launched in the 1930s. It might seem likely that the rise in the general standard of living will find expression in costly and perhaps elaborate possessions. But, conversely, it could happen that this same affluence in conjunction with mass-production and the so-called consumer mentality (meaning use-and-throw-way mentality) will greatly reduce people's emotional engagement with their belongings and result in continued anonymity of their appearance.

The circumstance likely to have the greatest influence on conditions is the population explosion. This, together with the demands for better living standards, will make such demands on production of houses and their furnishings as can only be met by a degree of rationalization hitherto unknown, and will allow little room, as far as details are concerned, for supplementary values connected with sentiment or opinions.

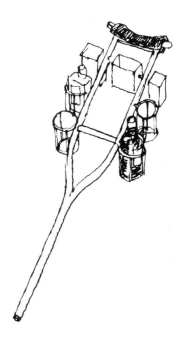

Heartless, pointless, immoral and
intolerably ugly

93

In other words, it will be less and less on individual things and more and more on the *whole* that the attention focuses. That will mean, for example, that chairs will become subordinate elements in relation to the room itself, if they do not disappear, indeed, to be replaced by cushions or by platforms that are part of the actual building. The first signs of this are already evident. In the same way houses will be subordinate in importance as personal architectural manifestations to the total image of the town. People are striving to control their environment. This control will tend more and more to include our treatment not only of our houses, streets and cities but also of the landscape and the way people live regionally. Pollution and conservation are as vital as design and may actually condition the design of our surroundings.

Making a virtue of necessity has always been one of the rules by which we judge the good-looking – we have at least that much common sense.

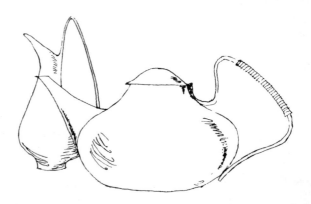